Vladimir Megre
The Ringing Cedars Series

English translation by John Woodsworth

- Book 1 **Anastasia**
  (ISBN 0-9763333-0-9)

- Book 2 **The Ringing Cedars of Russia**
  (ISBN 0-9763333-1-7)

- Book 3 **The Space of Love**
  (ISBN 0-9763333-2-5)

- Book 4 **Co-creation**
  (ISBN 0-9763333-3-3)

- Book 5 **Who Are We?**
  (ISBN 0-9763333-4-1)

- Book 6 **The Book of Kin**
  (ISBN 0-9763333-6-8)

- Book 7 **The Energy of Life**
  (ISBN 0-9763333-7-6)

- Book 8, Part 1 **The New Civilisation**
  (ISBN 0-9763333-8-4)

- Book 8, Part 2 **Rites of Love**
  (ISBN 0-9763333-9-2)

Published by **Ringing Cedars Press**
www.RingingCedars.com

I exist for those for whom I exist.
Anastasia

Anastasia herself has stated that this book, written about her, consists of words and phrases in combinations *which have a beneficial effect on the reader.* This has been attested by the letters received to date from thousands of readers all over the world.

If you wish to gain as full an appreciation as possible of the ideas, thoughts and images set forth here, as well as experience the benefits that come with this appreciation, we recommend you find a quiet place for your reading where there is the least possible interference from artificial noises (motor traffic, radio, TV, household appliances etc.). *Natural sounds,* on the other hand — the singing of birds, for example, or the patter of rain, or the rustle of leaves on nearby trees — may be a welcome accompaniment to the reading process.

Ringing Cedars Press is an independent publisher dedicated to making **Vladimir Megre**'s books available in the beautiful English translation by **John Woodsworth**. We rely on word of mouth as our only advertisement and thank all our readers for your help in spreading the message.

Order on-line   **www.RingingCedars.com**   ordering details
or call toll-free   **1-888-DOLMENS**   see last page

Generous discounts are available on volume orders. To help spread the word as a distributor or to place the books in your bookstore, please follow the **'Distribution'** link on our website or e-mail us at:

distrib@RingingCedars.com

Vladimir Megre

ANASTASIA

The Ringing Cedars Series
Book 1

Translated from the Russian by
John Woodsworth

Edited by
Leonid Sharashkin

Ringing Cedars Press
Columbia, Missouri, USA

Anastasia by
Vladimir Megre

Translation, Translator's Preface and footnotes by
John Woodsworth

Editing, Editor's Afterword, footnotes, design and layout by
Leonid Sharashkin

Cover art by
Alexander Razboinikov

Front cover font: *ShangriLaNF* by
Nick Curtis

Library of Congress Control Number 2004116185

ISBN 0-9763333-0-9

First edition, 2005

Published by
Ringing Cedars Press

www.RingingCedars.com

Contents

Translator's Preface

When I opened my on-line Slavic-languages bulletin one day in early September 2004 and first learnt about a book in the *Ringing Cedars Series* that was seeking a translator into English, little did I realise the kind of literary adventure that was awaiting me. But as I became acquainted with the details of Vladimir Megre's[1] fascinating work (I read through the first three books in the series before beginning the actual translation), it gradually dawned on me that much of my previous translation experience, especially in poetry (from Pushkin to Anna Akhmatova to modern bards) and poetic prose (as with the stories of contemporary Russian writer Mikhail Sadovsky), not to mention my own religious background (emphasising Man's unique status as the image and likeness of the Creator), had been preparing me specifically for this particular task. Megre's work was simply the next logical step, it seemed, in the progression of my career. Indeed, I found myself taking to it not only with the enthusiasm that comes with the prospect of facing a new professional challenge but even more with the thought of feeling very much at home in this new literary environment.

Some of my friends and colleagues have asked: "What kind of book are you translating?" — no doubt wondering whether they could look forward to reading a novel, a documentary account, an inspirational exegesis on the meaning of life, or even a volume of poetry.

But even after completing the translation of *Anastasia,* I still do not have a definitive answer to give them. In fact, I am still asking myself the same question.

---

[1]*Vladimir Megre* — pronounced *Vla-DEE-meer Mi-GREH* (capitalised syllables stressed). In fact, the pronunciation of the surname is not unlike that of its French counterpart, *Maigret.* The word *Anastasia* in Russian is sounded as *Ana-sta-SI-ya.*

My initial response was a rather crude summary of a gut impression — I would tell them: "Think of *Star Trek meets the Bible.*" My feelings about the book, however, go far beyond this primitive attempt at jocularity. Of the four disparate genres mentioned above, I would have to say *Anastasia* has elements of all four, and then some.

First — the book *reads* like a novel. That is to say, it tells a first-person story in a most entertaining way, bringing out the multi-faceted character of both the author and the title personage in a manner not unlike what readers of novels might expect. It tells a tale of adventure in the raw Siberian wilds where even sex and violence make an occasional appearance, though with a connection to the plot-line quite unlike their counterparts in any work of fiction I have read.

Secondly — the book gives the *impression* of a documentary account of real-life events, even if one's powers of belief are sometimes stretched to the limit. I am glad that my linguistic experience has given me access not only to the book itself, but also to a host of Russian-language texts on the Internet that have enabled me to corroborate from independent sources a great many of the specifics the author saw fit to include in his narrative (names of individuals, institutions, scientific phenomena etc.) — all of which turned out to be genuine, thereby contributing an additional measure of credence to what otherwise might seem utterly fantastic. Much of the corroborative information so gleaned I have attempted to pass on to the English-speaking reader in the footnotes, with the help of additional commentary by the publisher. And yet there is a significant area of the author's description where authenticity must still be judged by the individual reader (which to me is one of the hallmarks of a work of *literature,* in contrast to a merely academic or journalistic report).

Thirdly, the book *penetrates one's thinking and feelings* with the gentle force of a divinely-inspired treatise — a treatise on not only the meaning of human life, but much more. *Anastasia* offers a tremendous new insight into the whole interrelationship of God, Man, Nature and the Universe. I would even go so far as to call it a revelation in science and religion.

One 'nutshell' description that comes to my mind is *a chronicle of ideas* — ideas on (a) the history of humanity's relationship to everything outside itself, (b) the clouds (not only dark and foreboding but even the fluffy and attractive variety) of mistaken belief that have, over the years, hid this relationship from our sight and comprehension and (c) where to begin — once we have caught a glimpse of this relationship — the necessary journey to reclaiming the whole picture. Deeply metaphysical in essence, the chronicle is set forth with both the supporting evidence of a documentary account and the entertainment capacity of a novel. In other words, it can be read as any of these three in isolation, but only by taking the three dimensions together will the reader have something approaching a complete picture of the book. And all three are infused with a degree of soul-felt inspiration that can only be expressed in poetry.

Yes, indeed, one must not overlook the *poetry*. As a matter of fact, I learnt right at the start that experience in poetic translation was one of the qualifications required of a Ringing Cedars Series translator. And not just on account of the seven sample poems by readers at the end of Chapter 30.[2] Much of the book's prose (especially when Anastasia is speaking) exudes a poetic feel, with rhyme and metre running a background course through whole paragraphs at a time; hence a particular challenge lay in reproducing this poetic quality, along with the semantic meaning, in English translation. Such poetic prose is even more evident in subsequent books in the series.

Another challenge has been to match, as closely as possible, Vladimir Megre's progressive development as a writer. According to his own admission, Megre began this whole literary project not as a professional writer, but as a hardened entrepreneur for whom writing was the farthest activity from his mind.[3] I smiled when one of the test readers of the translation, after finishing the first few chapters, described the author's style as "choppy". Megre himself talks about the initial rejection notices he received from publisher after publisher, telling him his language was too "stilted".[4] And yet his

---

[2]These poems were written by readers with varying degrees of poetic experience. Every effort was made to reproduce the poetic features of the original (or, on occasion, their absence) on a poem-by-poem basis.

[3]See especially Chapters 15: "Attentiveness to Man" and 26: "Dreams — creating the future".

[4]See Chapter 30: "Author's message to readers".

rendering of some of Anastasia's pronouncements toward the end of Book I waxes quite lyrical indeed — especially in the poetic passages referred to above. The author's development in literary style (which he attributes to Anastasia's direct and indirect guidance) becomes even more pronounced as the series progresses. It will be up to the English-speaking reader to judge whether this transformation is also conveyed in the translation.

There were two Russian words, of frequent occurrence through-out the book, that presented a particular translation challenge. One of them was *dachniki* (plural of *dachnik*), referring to people who own a *dacha,* or a country cottage, situated on just 600 square metres of land obtainable free of charge from the Russian government. But there is little comparison here to most Western concepts of *cottagers.*[5] While Russian dachas may be found in forested areas, or simply on open farmland, one almost invariable feature is a plot (*uchastok*) on which are grown fruits and vegetables to supply the family not only for their dacha stays but right through the year.[6] Given that the word *dacha* is already known to many English speakers (and is included in popular editions of both Oxford and Webster), it was decided to use the Russian word designating its occupants as well, with the English plural ending: *dachniks.*

The question that entailed the most serious difficulty, however — one that formed the subject of several dozen e-mails between pub-lisher and translator before it was finally resolved — was the render-ing into English of the Russian word *chelovek*. It is the common term used to denote a person or a human being, the equivalent of German *Mensch* as well as of English *man* in the familiar Bible verse "God cre-ated man in His own image" (Genesis 1: 27).

---

[5] I am thinking especially here of the example I am most familiar with — namely, the 'cottage country' in the Muskoka Lakes region of Ontario, north of Toronto, dotted by vacation cottages with nothing but trees around and (in some cases) a view of a lake.

[6] According to official statistics, since entitlement to dachas was legalised in the 1960s, 35 million families (amounting to approximately 70% of Russia's total popu-lation!) have acquired these tiny parcels of land. The produce grown on these plots makes an enormous contribution to the national economy — for example, over 90% of the country's potatoes come from privately tended plots like these.

The problem with the term *human* (as in *human being*) is that it not only suggests a formation of the species from matter, or earth (compare: *humus* — the organic constituent of soil) but is associated with lowly concepts (from *humus* come words like *humble, humility* etc.),[7] whereas *chelovek* is derived from the old Russian words indicating 'thinking' (*chelo < lob*) and 'time' (*vek*) — i.e., an expression of man's dominion over time by virtue of his God-bestowed capacity for thinking and reason — not unlike the significance of *man* in the Bible verse cited above.

The problem with the word *man* is that, especially in our age, it has become so closely associated with only one half of the total number of sentient, thinking beings on the planet that the other half, quite understandably, feels collectively excluded by the term. Russian, by contrast, does not have this problem: *chelovek* can designate either a man or a woman.[8]

In the end, partly through reason and partly through revelation, it was decided to translate *chelovek,* wherever appropriate to the context, by the term *Man* with a capital *M,* in an effort to retain the association of the term with a divine as opposed to a material, earthly origin, as well as to show the link between Anastasia's view of Man (*chelovek*) and the concept of Man in the first chapter of Genesis, which she freely quotes herself. So let *all* readers of this book be put on notice: whenever you see *Man* with a capital *M,* this includes *you.*

There are other discrepancies between Russian and English concepts behind respective translation equivalents, but their explanation is best left to individual footnotes.

In conclusion, I must express my gratitude to my editor, Leonid Sharashkin of Ringing Cedars Press, first for entrusting me with the privileged task of translating such a monumental work as the

---

[7]Similarly, the word *person* is closely tied to its Latin root *persona*, signifying a *mask* — i.e., portraying a superficial appearance, rather than the inner essence of the individual. Interestingly enough, however, masks are sometimes deliberately used in theatre performances to suggest the thoughts and feelings of the character being portrayed.

[8]Russian does have a related problem, however: the word *chelovek* is *grammatically* masculine, even though its *meaning* is not confined to a single gender.

Ringing Cedars Series and, secondly, for the tremendous support he has given me throughout this initial project, namely, in illuminating aspects of Vladimir Megre's — and Anastasia's — concepts of God, Man, Nature and the Universe that my previous experience with Russian literature could not possibly have prepared me for. These shared insights have made a significant difference in how particular nuances of the original are rendered in the translation, and especially in making allowances for the considerable geographical, social and philosophical distances that all too often separate English-speaking readers from the vast cultural treasures accessible to those with a knowledge of Russian.

I now invite you all to take your seats in the familiar exploration vehicle known as the English language as we journey together to examine a previously inaccessible Russian treasure of momentous significance for all humanity (including the planet we collectively inhabit) — an experience summed up in one beautiful word: *Anastasia.*

Ottawa, Canada
January 2005   John Woodsworth

ANASTASIA

1

The ringing cedar

In the spring of 1994 I chartered three riverboats, on which I carried out a three-month expedition on the River Ob in Siberia, from Novosibirsk to Salekhard and back. The aim of the expedition was to foster economic ties with the regions of the Russian Far North.

The expedition went under the name of *The Merchant Convoy.* The largest of the three riverboats was a passenger ship named the *Patrice Lumumba.* (Western Siberian riverboats bear rather interesting names: the *Maria Ulyanova,* the *Patrice Lumumba,* the *Mikhail Kalinin,*[1] as if there were no other personages in history worth commemorating.) The lead ship *Patrice Lumumba* housed the expedition headquarters, along with a store where local Siberian entrepreneurs could exhibit their wares.

The plan was for the convoy to travel north 3,500 kilometres,[2] visiting not only major ports of call such as Tomsk, Nizhnevartovsk, Khanty-Mansiysk and Salekhard, but smaller places as well, where goods could be unloaded only during a brief summer navigation season.

The convoy would dock at a populated settlement during the daytime. We would offer the wares we had brought for sale and hold talks about setting up regular economic links. Our travelling was

---

[1]*Maria Ulyanova* — a name borne by two historical figures: *Maria Alexandrovna Ulyanova* (*née* Blank, 1835–1916) — mother to Vladimir Ilich Ulyanov (a.k.a. Vladimir Lenin, founder of the Soviet Union), and *Maria Ilinichna Ulyanova* (1878–1937) — Lenin's sister; the ship has since been re-named the *Viktor Gashkov. Patrice Emery Lumumba* (1925–1961) — Communist leader of the *Mouvement National Congolais*, who formed the first elected government of the Democratic Republic of the Congo; the ship is now known as the *Paris. Mikhail Ivanovich Kalinin* (1875–1946) — as Chairman of the Soviet National Executive Committee, the USSR's first titular Head of State; the *Kalinin* still retains its original name.

[2]*3,500 kilometres* — The metric system of measures is used throughout the book. One kilometre equals approximately six tenths (0.6) of a mile.

usually done at night. If weather conditions were unfavourable for navigation, the lead ship would put into the nearest port, and we would organise on-board parties for the local young people. Most places offered little in the way of their own entertainment. Clubs and community centres (so-called 'Houses of Culture') had been going downhill ever since the collapse of the USSR, and there were almost no cultural activities available.

Sometimes we might go for twenty-four hours or more without seeing a single populated place, even the tiniest village. From the river — the only transportation artery for many kilometres around — the only thing visible to the eye was the taiga[3] itself. I was not yet aware at the time that somewhere amidst the uninhabited vastness of forest along the riverbank a surprise meeting was awaiting me — one that was to change my whole life.

One day on our way back to Novosibirsk, I arranged to dock the lead ship at a small village, one with only a few houses at best, some thirty or forty kilometres distant from the larger population centres. I planned a three-hour stopover so the crew could have shore leave and the local residents could buy some of our goods and foodstuffs and we could cheaply pick up from them fish and wild-growing plants of the taiga.

During our stopover time, as the leader of the expedition I was approached by two of the local senior citizens (as I judged at the time) — one of them appeared to be somewhat older than the other. The elder of the two — a wisened fellow with a long grey beard — kept silent the whole time, leaving his younger companion to do the talking. This fellow tried to persuade me to lend him fifty of my crew (which numbered no more than sixty-five in total) to go with them into the taiga, about twenty-five kilometres or so from the dock where the ship was berthed. They would be taken into the depths of the taiga to cut down a tree he described as a 'ringing cedar'.[4] The

---

[3]*taiga* — the Russian name given to the boreal forest that stretches across much of Siberia and northern Canada. The word *Siberia* is derived from an Old Tungus word *sivir* meaning 'land', 'world' or 'tribe'.

[4]*cedar* (Russian *kedr*) — in this case (and throughout the book) referring to either the Siberian pine (Siberian cedar, *Pinus sibirica*) or to the Lebanese cedar (*Cedrus libani*).

cedar, which he said reached forty metres in height,[5] needed to be cut up into pieces which could be carried by hand to the ship. We must, he said, definitely take the whole lot.

The old fellow further recommended that each piece be cut up into smaller pieces. Each of us should keep one for himself and give the rest to relatives, friends and anyone who wished to accept a piece as a gift. He said this was a most unusual cedar. The piece should be worn on one's chest as a pendant. Hang it around your neck while standing barefoot in the grass, and then press it to your chest with the palm of your left hand. It takes only a moment to feel the pleasing warmth emanating from the piece of cedar, followed by a light tingling sensation running through the whole body. From time to time, whenever desired, the side of the pendant facing away from the body should be rubbed with one's fingers, the thumbs pressed against the other side. The old fellow confidently assured me that within three months the possessor of one of these 'ringing cedar' pendants will feel significant improvement in his sense of well-being, and will be cured of many diseases.

"Even AIDS?" I asked, and briefly explained what I had learnt about this disease from the press.

The oldster confidently replied:

"From any and all diseases!"

But this, he considered, was an easy task. The main benefit was that anyone having one of these pendants would become kinder, more successful and more talented.

I did know a little about the healing properties of the cedars of our Siberian taiga, but the suggestion that it could affect one's feelings and abilities — well, that to me seemed beyond the bounds of probability. The thought came to me that maybe these old men wanted money from me for this 'unusual cedar', as they themselves called it. And I began explaining that out in 'the big wide world', women were used to wearing jewellery made of gold and silver and wouldn't pay a dime for some scrap of wood, and so I wasn't going to lay out any money for anything like that.

---

[5] *forty metres* — about 131 feet. The *metre* is the basic unit of length in the metric system, equal to 3.28 feet.

"They don't know what they're wearing," came the reply. "Gold — well, that's dust in comparison with one piece of this cedar. But we don't need any money for it. We can give you some dried mushrooms in addition, but there's nothing we need from you..."

Not wanting to start an argument, out of respect for their age, I said:

"Well, maybe someone will wear some of your cedar pendants. They certainly would if a top wood-carving craftsman agreed to put his hand to it and create something of amazing beauty!"

To which the old fellow replied:

"Yes, you could carve it, but it would be better to polish it by rubbing. It will be a lot better if you do this yourself, with your fingers, whenever your heart desires — then the cedar will also have a beautiful look to it."

Then the younger of the two quickly unbuttoned first his old worn jacket and then his shirt and revealed what he was wearing on his chest. I looked and saw a puffed-out circle or oval. It was multi-coloured — purple, raspberry, auburn — forming some kind of puzzling design — the vein-lines on the wood looked like little streams. I am not a connoisseur of *objets d'art*, although from time to time I have had occasion to visit picture galleries. The world's great masters had not called forth any particular emotions in me, but the object hanging around this man's neck aroused significantly greater feelings and emotions than any of my visits to the Tretyakov Gallery.[6]

"How many years have you been rubbing this piece of cedar?" I asked.

"Ninety-three," the old fellow responded.

"And how old are you?"

"A hundred and nineteen."

At the time I didn't believe him. He looked like a man of seventy-five. Either he hadn't noticed my doubts or, if he had, he paid no attention to them. In somewhat excited tones he started in trying to persuade me that any piece of this cedar, polished by human fingers

---

[6]*Tretyakov Gallery* — the foremost collection of Russian art in the world, located in the centre of Moscow. The original collector, Pavel Tretyakov, donated his extensive collection to the City of Moscow in 1892; it has been steadily increasing ever since.

alone, would also look beautiful in just three years. Then it would start looking even better and better, especially when worn by a woman. The body of its wearer would give off a pleasant and beneficial aroma, quite unlike anything artificially produced by Man!

Indeed, a very pleasant fragrance was emanating from both these old men. I could feel it, even though I'm a smoker and (like all smokers) have a dulled sense of smell.

And there was one other peculiarity...

I suddenly became aware of phrases in the speech of these strangers that were not common to the residents of this isolated part of the North. Some of them I remember to this day, even the intonations associated with them. Here is what the old fellow told me:

"God created the cedar to store cosmic energy...

"When someone is in a state of love they emit a radiant energy. It takes but a second for it to reflect off the celestial bodies floating overhead and come back to Earth and give life to everything that breathes.

"The Sun is one of those celestial bodies, and it reflects but a tiny fraction of such radiance.

"Only bright rays can travel into Space from Man on the Earth. And only beneficial rays can be reflected from Space back to Earth.

"Under the influence of malicious feelings Man can emit only dark rays. These dark rays cannot rise but must fall into the depths of the Earth. Bouncing off its core, they return to the surface in the form of volcanic eruptions, earthquakes, wars etc.

"The culminating achievement of these dark rays is their direct effect on the Man originating them, invariably exacerbating this Man's own malicious feelings.

"Cedars live to be five hundred and fifty years old. Day and night their millions of needles catch and store the whole spectrum of bright energy.[7] During the period of the cedars' life all the celestial bodies pass above them, reflecting this bright energy.

---

[7]Trees indeed capture a wide range of radiation beyond visible light. Man-made antennas are but an imitation of branching pattern in trees. Both the structure of trees and the materials composing them betray natural wave-receptors. Tree sap is a great conductor of electricity (this is why a tree hit by a lightning virtually explodes), and

"Even in one tiny piece of cedar there is more energy beneficial to Man than in all the man-made energy installations taken together.

"Cedars receive the energy emanating from Man through Space, store it up and at the right moment give it back. They give it back when there is not enough of it in Space — in other words, in Man — or in everything living and growing on the Earth.

"Occasionally, though very rarely, one discovers cedars that have been storing up energy but not giving back what they have stored. After five hundred years of their life they start to ring. This is how they talk to us, through their quiet ringing sound — this is how they signal people to take them and saw them up to make use of their stored-up energy on the Earth. This is what the cedars are asking with their ringing sound. They keep on asking for three whole years. If they don't have contact with living human beings, then in three years, deprived of the opportunity to give back what they have received and stored from Space, they lose their ability to give it back directly to Man. Then they will start burning up the energy internally. This torturous process of burning and dying lasts twenty-seven years.

"Not long ago we discovered a cedar like this. We determined that it had been ringing for two years already. It was ringing very softly. Perhaps it is trying to draw out its request over a longer period of time, but still, it has only one year left. It must be sawed up and given away to people."

The old man spoke at length, and for some reason I heard him out. The voice of this strange old *Sibiriak*[8] sounded at first quietly confident, then very excited, and when he got excited, he would rub the piece of cedar with his fingertips as though they were lightly tripping over some kind of musical instrument.

---

static electricity was first received from *amber* — a fossil resin from conifer trees. For details please see Dr Philip Callahan's books, including *Tuning in to nature* and *Ancient mysteries, modern visions: The magnetic life of agriculture*. Viktor Schauberger (see footnote 1 in Chapter 16: "Flying saucers? Nothing extraordinary!") referred to trees as "bioelectric condensers". This statement is corroborated by Dr Georges Lakhovsky (see footnote 2 in Chapter 26: "Dreams — creating the future"), a pioneer explorer of energy fields as the foundation of all life on a cellular level.

[8] *Sibiriak* — the Russian word denoting a resident of Siberia.

It was cold on the riverbank. An autumn wind was blowing across the river. Gusts of wind ruffled the hair on the old men's capless heads, but the spokesman's jacket and shirt remained unbuttoned. His fingertips kept rubbing the cedar pendant on his chest, still exposed to the wind. He was still trying to explain its significance to me.

Lidia Petrovna,[9] an employee of my firm, came down the gangplank to tell me that everyone else was already on board and waiting for me to finish my conversation. I bade farewell to the oldsters and quickly climbed aboard. I couldn't act on their request — for two reasons: delaying departure, especially for three days, would mean a significant financial loss. And besides, everything these old fellows said seemed to me, at the time, to be in the realm of pure superstition.

The next morning during our usual company meeting I suddenly noticed that Lidia Petrovna was fingering a cedar pendant of her own. Later she would tell me that after I'd gone aboard she stayed behind for a while. She noticed that when I started hurrying away from them, the oldster that had been talking with me stared after me with a perplexed look, and then said excitedly to his older companion:

"Now how can that be? Why didn't they get it? I really don't know how to speak their language. I couldn't make them believe, I simply couldn't! Why? Tell me, Father!"

The elder man put his hand on his son's shoulder and replied:

"You weren't convincing enough, son! They didn't grasp it."

"As I was going up the gangplank," Lidia Petrovna went on, "the old man that was talking with you suddenly rushed up to me, grabbed me by the arm, and led me back down to the grass below.

"He hurriedly pulled out of his pocket a string, and attached to it was this piece of cedar wood. He put it around my neck, and pressed it against my chest with the palm of both his hand and mine. I even felt a shiver go through my whole body. Somehow he managed to do all this very quickly, and I didn't even get a chance to say anything to him.

---

[9]*Lidia Petrovna* — *Petrovna* here is a patronymic, derived from her father's first name (*Petr,* pronounce 'Piotr'). The combination of the first name plus the patronymic is the standard form of formal address among business colleagues and acquaintances.

"As I was walking away, he called after me: 'Have a safe journey! Be happy! Please come again next year! All the best, people! We'll be waiting for you! Have a safe journey!'

"As the ship pulled away from the dock, the old fellow kept on waving at us for a long time, and then all at once sat down on the grass. I was watching him through a pair of binoculars. The old man that talked with you and later gave me the pendant — I saw him sit down on the grass, and his shoulders were trembling. The older one with the long beard was bending over him and stroking his head."

Amidst the flurry of my subsequent commercial dealings, account-keeping and end-of-voyage farewell banquets I completely forgot about the strange Siberian oldsters.

Upon my return to Novosibirsk I was afflicted with sharp pains. The diagnosis: a duodenal intestinal ulcer and osteochondrosis of the thoracic spine.

In the quiet of the comfy hospital ward I was cut off from the bustle of everyday life. My deluxe private room gave me an opportunity to calmly reflect on my four-month expedition and to draw up a business plan for the future. But it seemed as though my memory relegated just about everything that had happened to the background and for some reason the old men and what they said came to the forefront of my thought.

I requested to have delivered to me in the hospital all sorts of literature on cedars. After comparing what I read with what I had heard, I became more and more amazed and began to actually believe what the oldsters had said. There was at least some kind of truth in their words... or maybe the whole thing was true?!

In books on folk medicine there is a lot said about the cedar as a healing remedy. They say that everything from the tips of the needles to the bark is endowed with highly effective healing properties. The Siberian cedar wood has a beautiful appearance, and artistic wood-carving masters enjoy great success in using it for furniture as well as soundboards for musical instruments. Cedar needles are highly capable of decontaminating the surrounding air. Cedar wood has a distinctive, pleasant balsam fragrance. A small cedar chip placed inside a house will keep moths away.

In the popular-science literature I read it was said that the qualitative characteristics for the northern cedars were significantly higher than for those growing in the south.

Back in 1792 the academician P.S. Pallas[10] wrote that the fruits of the Siberian cedar were effective in restoring youth and virility and significantly increasing the body's ability to withstand a number of diseases.

There is a whole host of historical phenomena directly or indirectly linked to the Siberian cedar. Here is one of them.

In 1907 a fifty-year-old semi-literate peasant named Gregory Rasputin,[11] who hailed from an isolated Siberian village in an area where the Siberian cedar grows, found himself in St. Petersburg, the capital, and soon became a regular guest of the imperial family. Not only did he amaze them with his predictions, but he possessed incredible sexual stamina. At the time of his assassination, onlookers were struck by the fact that despite his bullet-ridden body he continued to live. Perhaps because he had been raised on cedar nuts in a part of the country where cedars abound?

This is how a contemporary journalist described his staying power:

"At age fifty he could begin an orgy at noon and go on carousing until four o'clock in the morning. From his fornication and drunkenness he would go directly to the church for morning prayers and stand

---

[10]*P.S. Pallas* — a reference to Peter Simon Pallas (1741–1811), a German zoologist, paleontologist, botanist and ethnographer, born in St. Petersburg. As a member of the St. Petersburg Academy of Sciences, he was a prominent pioneer explorer of the Siberian taiga.

[11]*Gregory Efimovich Rasputin* (1871?–1916; sources do not agree on the date of his birth) — a monk from the Tiumen region of Western Siberia who appeared to have unusual healing powers. He curried favour with the court of Tsar Nicholas I (especially Nicholas' wife Alexandra Fedorovna) by demonstrating a beneficial influence on their son (and heir to the throne) Alexei, who suffered from hemophilia.

praying until eight, before heading home for a cup of tea. Then, as if nothing had happened, he would carry on receiving visitors until two in the afternoon. Next he would collect a group of ladies and accompany them to the baths. From the baths he would be off to a restaurant in the country, where he would begin repeating the previous night's activities. No normal person could ever keep up a régime like that."

The many-time world champion and Olympic champion wrestler Alexander Karelin, who has never been defeated so far,[12] is also a Siberian, also from an area where the Siberian cedar grows. This strongman also eats cedar nuts. A co-incidence?

I mention only those facts which can be easily verified in popular-science literature, or which can be confirmed by witnesses. Lidia Petrovna, who was given the 'ringing cedar' pendant by the Siberian oldster, is now one of those witnesses. She is thirty-six years old, married with two children. Her co-workers have noticed changes in her behaviour. She has become kinder and smiles more often. Her husband, whom I happen to know, told me that their family has now been experiencing a greater degree of mutual understanding. He also remarked that his wife has somehow become younger-looking, and is starting to arouse greater feelings in him — more respect and, quite possibly, more love.

But all these multitudinous facts and evidences pale in comparison to the main point, which you can look up for yourself — a discovery which has left me with not a trace of doubt — and that is the *Bible*. In the Book of Leviticus in the Old Testament (Ch. 14, vs. 4), God teaches us how to treat people, and even decontaminate their houses, with the help of... the *cedar!!!*

After comparing all the facts and data I had gleaned from various sources, I was confronted by such a remarkable picture that all the miracles known to the world faded before it. The great mysteries that have excited people's minds began to pale into insignificance

---

[12] *Alexander Alexandrovich Karelin* (1967–) — a Russian, European, Olympic and world champion wrestler many times over, undefeated in international competition from 1987 to 2000 (for most of this time not even giving up a point).

in comparison with the mystery of the ringing cedar. Now I could no longer have any doubts about its existence. They were all dispelled by the popular-science literature and the Old Vedic scriptures I was reading.

Cedars are mentioned forty-two times in the Bible, all in the Old Testament.[13] When Moses presented humanity with the Ten Commandments on stone tablets, he probably knew more than has been recorded in the Old Testament.

We are accustomed to the fact that in Nature there are various plants capable of treating human ills. The healing properties of the cedar have been attested in popular-science literature by such serious and authoritative researchers as Academician Pallas, and this is consistent with the Old Testament scriptures.

And now, pay careful attention!

When the Old Testament talks about the cedar, it is just the cedar alone; nothing is said about other trees.[14] And doesn't the Old Testament say that the cedar is the most potent medicine of any existing in Nature? What is this, anyway? A medicine kit? And how is it to be used? And why, out of all the Siberian cedars, did these strange old fellows point to a single 'ringing cedar'?

But that's not all. Something immeasurably more mysterious lies behind this story from the Old Testament:

King Solomon built a temple out of cedar wood. In return for the cedar from Lebanon, he gave another king, Hiram, twenty cities of his kingdom. Incredible! Giving away twenty cities just for some kind of building materials?! True, he got something else in return. At King Solomon's request he was given servants that were "skilled in felling timber".[15]

What kind of people were these? What knowledge did they possess?

---

[13] In the *Authorised (King James) Version* of the English Bible, in fact, the word *cedar* (or *cedars*) appears 75 times, from Leviticus to Zechariah.

[14] There are of course, separate references in the Bible to a number of trees (e.g., fir, oak, juniper), but not in conjunction with cedars.

[15] I Kings 5: 6 (*New International Version*).

I have heard that even now, in the far-flung reaches of the taiga there are old people whose job it is to choose trees for construction. But back then, over two thousand years ago, everybody might have known this. Nevertheless, specialists of some sort were required. The temple was built. Services began to be held there, and... "the priests could not stand to minister because of the cloud".[16]

What kind of a cloud was that? How and from where did it enter the temple? What could it have been? Energy? A spirit? What kind of phenomenon, and what connection did it have with the cedar?

The old fellows talked about the ringing cedar as storing up some kind of energy.

Which cedars are stronger — the ones in Lebanon or Siberia?

Academician Pallas said that the healing properties of the cedars increased in proportion to their proximity to the forest tundra. In that case, then, the Siberian cedar would be the stronger.

It says in the Bible: "...by their fruits ye shall know them."[17] In other words, again the Siberian cedar!

Could it be that no one has paid any attention to all this?

Has no one put two and two together?

The Old Testament, the science of the past century and the current one — are all of the same opinion regarding the cedar.

And Elena Ivanovna Roerich[18] notes in her book *Living ethics*: "...a chalice of cedar resin figured in the rituals of the consecration of the kings of the ancient Khorassan. Druids also called the chalice of cedar resin the Chalice of Life. And only later, with the loss of the realization of the spirit, was it replaced by blood. The fire of Zoroaster was the result of burning of the cedar resin in the chalice."[19]

---

[16] I Kings 8: 11 (*Authorised King James Version*).

[17] Matth. 7: 20 (*Authorised King James Version*).

[18] *Elena Ivanovna Roerich [Rerikh]* (1879–1955) — Russian religious thinker. Travelling through Asia with her husband, the prominent Russian artist Nikolai Konstantinovich Roerich, she became fascinated with Oriental religions and devoted her career to studying and writing about them. In 1920 she and her husband founded the Agni Yoga Society, a non-profit educational institution in New York.

[19] This translation is taken from an English version of Roerich's *Leaves of Morya's Garden, Book 2: Illumination* (1925) — 2.4.18.

So, then, how much of our forebears' knowledge of the cedar, its properties and uses has been passed down to the present day?

Is it possible that nothing has been preserved?

What do the Siberian oldsters know about it?

And all at once my memory harked back to an experience of many years ago, which caused a shiver to run up and down my spine. I didn't pay any attention to it back then, but now...

During the early years of *perestroika* I was president of the Association of Siberian Entrepreneurs. One day I got a call from the Novosibirsk District Executive Council (back then we still had Communist Party committees and 'Executive Councils'), asking me to come to a meeting with a prominent Western businessman. He had a letter of recommendation from the government of the day. Several entrepreneurs were present, along with workers from the Executive Council secretariat.

The 'Western businessman' was of a rather imposing external appearance — an unusual person with Oriental features. He was wearing a turban, and his fingers were adorned with precious rings.

The discussion, as usual, centred around the possibilities for cooperation in various fields. The visitor said, among other things: "We would like to buy cedar nuts from you." As he spoke these words, his face and body tightened, and his sharp eyes moved from side to side, no doubt studying the reaction of the entrepreneurs present. I remember the incident very well, as even then I wondered why his appearance had changed like that.

After the official meeting the Moscow interpreter accompanying him came up to me. She said he would like to speak with me.

The businessman made me a confidential proposal: if I could arrange delivery of cedar nuts for him — and they had to be fresh — then I would receive a handsome personal percentage over and above the official price.

The nuts were to be shipped to Turkey for processing into some kind of oil. I said I would think it over.

I decided I would find out for myself what kind of oil he was talking about. And I did...

On the London market, which sets the standard for world prices, cedar nut oil fetches anywhere up to five hundred dollars per kilogram![20] Their proposed deal would have given us approximately two to three dollars for one kilogram of cedar nuts.

I rang up an entrepreneur I happened to know in Warsaw, and asked him whether it might be possible to market such a product directly to the consumer, and whether we could learn the technology involved in its extraction.

A month later he sent me a reply: "No way. We weren't able to gain access to the technology. And besides, there are certain Western powers so involved in these issues of yours that it would be better just to forget about it."

After that I turned to my good friend, Konstantin Rakunov,[21] a scholar with our Novosibirsk Consumer Co-operative Institute. I bought a shipment of nuts and financed a study. And the laboratories of his institute produced approximately 100 kilograms of cedar nut oil.

I also hired researchers, who came up with the following information from archival documents:

Before the Revolution (and even for some time afterward) there was in Siberia an organisation known as the *Siberian Co-operator.* People from this organisation traded in oil, including cedar nut oil. They had rather swanky branch offices in Harbin, London and New York and rather large Western bank accounts.[22] After the revolution the organisation eventually collapsed, and many of its members went abroad.

A member of the Bolshevist government, Leonid Krasin,[23] met with the head of this organisation and asked him to return to Russia.

---

[20]*kilogram* — metric measure of weight, equal to approximately 2.2 pounds.

[21]*Konstantin Petrovich Rakunov* (1954–), with a post-graduate degree in economics, holds the rank of *docent* (equivalent to Associate Professor) in the Management Department at what is now the Novosibirsk Consumer Co-operative University; he is the author of a number of scholarly publications on consumer co-operatives.

[22]In fact, prior to the 1917 revolution Russian exports of cedar nut oil generated 10% of all foreign-trade revenues, rivalling such commodities as grain, timber and furs.

[23]*Leonid Borisovich Krasin* (1870–1928) — an early Bolshevik and Communist Party activist. During the 1920s he served as Foreign Trade minister as well as the new government's trade representative in London and Paris.

But the head of the *Siberian Co-operator* replied that he would be of more help to Russia if he remained outside its borders.

From archival materials I further learnt that cedar oil was made using wooden (only wooden!) presses in many villages of the Siberian taiga. The quality of the cedar oil depended on the season in which the nuts were gathered and how they were processed. But I was unable to determine, either from the archives or the institute, exactly which season was being indicated. The secret had been lost. There are no healing remedies with properties analogous to those of cedar oil. But perhaps the secret of making this oil had been passed along by one of the émigrés to someone in the West? How was it possible that the cedar nuts with the most effective healing properties grow in Siberia, and yet the facility for producing the oil is located in Turkey? After all, Turkey has no cedars like those found in Siberia.

And just what 'Western powers' was the Warsaw entrepreneur talking about? Why did he say it would be better just to forget about this issue? Might not these powers be 'smuggling' this product with its extraordinary healing properties out of our Russian-Siberian taiga? Why, with such a treasure here at home with such effective properties, a treasure known for centuries — for millennia, even, do we spend millions and maybe billions of dollars buying up foreign medicines and swallow them up like half-crazed people? How is it that we have lost the knowledge known to our forebears? Our recent forebears yet — ones who lived in our century!

And what about the Bible's description of that extraordinary happening of over two thousand years ago? What kind of unknown powers are trying so earnestly to erase our forebears' knowledge from our own memories? "Oh, you'd better stick to minding your own business!" we're told. Yes, they *are* trying to wipe it out. And, indeed, they are succeeding!

I was seized by a fit of anger. I checked, and yes, cedar oil *is* sold in our pharmacies, but it is sold in foreign packaging! I bought a single thirty-gram vial and tried it. The actual oil content, I think, was no more than a couple of drops — the rest was some kind of diluting agent. Compared to what was produced in the Consumer Co-operative Institute — well, there was simply no comparison. And these diluted couple of drops cost fifty thousand roubles![24] So what if we didn't buy it abroad, but sold it ourselves? Just the sale of this oil would be enough to raise the whole of Siberia above the poverty level! But how did we ever manage to let go of the technology of our forebears?! And here we are snivelling that we live like paupers...

Well, okay, I think I'll come up with something all the same. I'll produce the oil myself — and my firm will only get wealthier.

I decided I would try a second expedition along the Ob — back up north, using only my headquarters ship, the *Patrice Lumumba*. I loaded a variety of goods for sale into the hold, and turned the film-viewing room into a store. I decided to hire a new crew and not invite anyone from my firm. As things stood, my firm's financial situation had worsened while I was distracted with my new interest.

Two weeks after leaving Novosibirsk my security guards reported they had overheard conversations about the ringing cedar. And, in their opinion, the newly hired workers included some 'pretty strange people', to put it mildly. I began summoning individual crew members to my quarters to talk about the forthcoming trek into the taiga. Some of them even agreed to go on a volunteer basis. Others asked for extra pay for this operation, since it was not something they had agreed to when signing up for work. It was one thing to stay in the comfortable conditions aboard ship — quite another to trek twenty-five kilometres into the taiga and back, carrying loads of wood. My finances at the time were already pretty tight. I had not planned on selling the cedar. After all, the oldsters had said it should be given away. Besides, my main interest was not the cedar tree itself, but the secret of how to extract the oil. And of course it would be fascinating to find out all the details connected with it.

Little by little, with the help of my security guards, I realised that there would be attempts made to spy on my movements, especially after I left the ship. But for what purpose was unclear. And who was behind the would-be spies? I thought and thought about it, and decided that to be absolutely certain, I would somehow have to outsmart everyone at once.

_____

[24]*fifty thousand roubles* — approximately 16 US dollars at the November 1994 exchange rate — equivalent to 20% of the average Russian's monthly income.

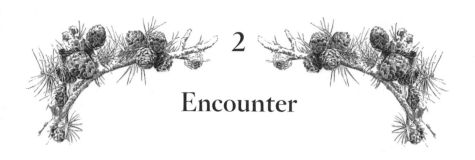

2

Encounter

Without a word to anyone, I arranged to have the ship stop not far from the place where I had met the old men the previous year. Then I took a small motorboat and reached the village. I gave orders to the captain to continue along the trade route.

I hoped I would be able, with the help of the local residents, to look up the two old fellows, see the ringing cedar with my own eyes and determine the cheapest way of getting it back to the ship. Tying the motorboat to a rock on the shore, I was about to head for one of the little houses close by. But spotting a woman standing alone on the riverbank, I decided to approach her.

The woman had on an old quilted jacket, long skirt and high rubber galoshes of the kind worn by many residents of the northern backwoods during the spring and fall. On her head was a kerchief tied so that the forehead and neck were fully covered. It was hard to tell just how old this woman was. I said hello and told her about the two old men I had met here the previous year.

"It was my grandfather and great-grandfather who talked with you here last year, Vladimir," the woman replied.

I was amazed. Her voice sounded very young, her diction was crystal clear. She called me by my first name and right off used the informal form of address.[1] I couldn't remember the names of the oldsters, or whether we had introduced ourselves at all. I thought now we must have done so, since this woman knew my name. I asked her (deciding to continue in the same informal tone):

"And how do you call yourself?"

"Anastasia", the woman answered, stretching out her hand toward me, palm down, as though expecting me to kiss it.

This gesture of a country woman in a quilted jacket and galoshes, standing on a deserted shore and trying to act like a lady of the world, amused me no end. I shook her hand. Naturally, I wasn't going to kiss it. Anastasia gave me an embarrassed smile and suggested I go with her into the taiga, to where her family lived.

"The only thing is, we'll have to make our way through the taiga, twenty-five kilometres. That's not too much for you?"

"Well, of course, it's rather far. But can you show me the ringing cedar?"

"Yes, I can."

"You know all about that, you'll tell me?"

"I shall tell you what I know."

"Then let's go!"

Along the way Anastasia told me how their family, their kin, had been living in the cedar forest generation after generation — as her forebears had said, over the course of several millennia. It is only extremely rarely that they find themselves in direct contact with people from our civilised society. These contacts do not occur in their places of permanent residence, but only when they come into the villages under the guise of hunters or travellers from some other settlement. Anastasia herself had been to two big cities: Tomsk and Moscow. But only for one day each. Not even to stay the night. She wanted to see whether she might have been mistaken in her perceptions about the lifestyle of city people. She had saved the money for the trip by selling berries and dried mushrooms. A local village woman had lent her her passport.[2]

Anastasia did not approve of her grandfather and great-grandfather's idea of giving away the ringing cedar with its healing properties to a whole lot of people. When asked why, she replied that the pieces of cedar would be scattered among evildoers as well as good people. In all probability the majority of the pieces would be snatched up by

---

[2]*passport* — in this case, an internal identity document required for any kind of travel within the Russian Federation (or the former Soviet Union).

negative-thinking individuals. In the final analysis they might end up doing more harm than good. The most important thing, in her opinion, was to promote the good. And to help people through whom the good was accomplished. If everyone were benefited at random, the imbalance between good and evil would not be changed, but would stay the same or even get worse.

After my encounter with the Siberian oldsters I looked through a variety of popular-science literature along with a host of historical and scholarly works describing the unusual properties of the cedar. Now I was trying to penetrate and comprehend what Anastasia was saying about the lifestyle of the cedar people and thinking to myself: "Now what if anything can that be compared to?"

I thought about the Lykovs[3] — a true story many Russians are familiar with from the account by Vasily Peskov of another family that lived an isolated life for many years in the taiga. They were written up in the paper *Komsomolskaya Pravda* under the headline: "Dead-end in the taiga", and were the subject of television programmes. I had formulated for myself an impression of the Lykovs as people who knew Nature pretty well, but had a rather fuzzy concept of our modern civilised life. But this was a different situation. Anastasia gave the impression of someone who was perfectly acquainted with our life and with something else besides that I couldn't fathom at all. She was quite at ease discussing our city life, she seemed to know it first-hand.

We walked along, getting deeper into the woods, and after about five kilometres stopped to rest. At this point she took off her jacket, kerchief and long skirt, and placed them in the hollow of a tree. All she was wearing now was a short, light-weight frock. I was dumbstruck at what I saw. If I were a believer in miracles, I would put this down to something like extreme metamorphosis.

For now here before me stood a very young woman with long golden hair and a fantastic figure. Her beauty was most unusual. It

---

[3]*the Lykovs* — a family of 'Old Believers' that lived in self-imposed isolation in the taiga unknown to the outside world through most of the Soviet period. They were discovered by a party of geologists in 1978. Their story is told by *Komsomolskaya Pravda* journalist Vasily Peskov in his book *Lost in the taiga* (available in English translation).

would be hard to imagine how any of the winners of the world's most prestigious beauty contests could rival her appearance, or, as it later turned out, her intellectual prowess. Everything about this taiga girl was alluring, simply spellbinding.

"You are probably tired?" asked Anastasia. "Would you like to rest for a while?"

We sat down right on the grass, and I was able to get a closer look at her face. There were no cosmetics covering her perfect features. Her lovely well-toned skin bore no resemblance to the weather-beaten faces of people I knew who lived in the Siberian backwoods. Her large greyish-blue eyes had a kindly look, and her lips betrayed a gentle smile. As indicated, she wore a short, light-weight smock, something like a night-shirt, at the same time giving the impression that her body was not at all cold, in spite of the 12–15-degree temperatures.[4]

I decided to have a bite to eat. I reached into my bag and took out sandwiches, along with a travel bottle filled with good cognac. I offered to share it with Anastasia but she refused the cognac and for some reason even declined to eat with me. While I was snacking, Anastasia lay on the grass, her eyes blissfully closed, as though inviting the sun's rays to caress her. The rays reflected off her upturned palms with a golden glow. Lying there half-exposed, she appeared absolutely gorgeous!

I looked at her and thought to myself: "Now why do women always bare to the limit either their legs, or their breasts, or everything at once with their mini-skirts and décolletage? Is it not to appeal to the men around them, as if to say: "Look how charming I am, how open and accessible!" And what are men obliged to do then? Fight against their fleshly passions and thereby denigrate women with their lack of attention? Or make advances toward them and thereby break a God-given law?"

When I had finished eating, I asked:

---

[4]*12–15 degree temperatures* — the Celsius (Centigrade) scale common throughout Russia, Europe and Canada, is used throughout the book. 12–15 degrees Celsius equals 54–59 degrees Fahrenheit. To convert a Celsius temperature to Fahrenheit, multiply it by 1.8 and add 32.

"Anastasia, you're not afraid of walking through the taiga alone?"

"There is nothing I have to fear here," replied Anastasia.

"Interesting, but how would you defend yourself if you happened to encounter two or three burly men — geologists, or hunters, let's say?"

She didn't answer, only smiled.

I thought: "How is it that this so extraordinarily alluring young beauty could not be afraid of anyone or anything?"

What happened next still makes me feel uncomfortable, even to this day. I grabbed her by her shoulders and pulled her close to me. She didn't offer any strong resistance, although I could feel a considerable degree of strength in her resilient body. The last thing I remember before losing consciousness was her saying: "Do not do this... Calm down!" And even before that I remember being suddenly overcome by a powerful attack of fear. A fear of what, I couldn't grasp — as sometimes happens in childhood when you find yourself at home all alone and suddenly become afraid of something.

When I woke up, she was on her knees, bending over me. One hand lay upon my chest, while the other was waving to someone up above, or to either side. She was smiling, though not at me, but rather, it seemed, at someone who was invisibly surrounding us or above us. Anastasia seemed to be literally gesturing to her invisible friend that there was nothing amiss going on. Then she calmly and tenderly looked me in the eye:

"Calm down, Vladimir, it is over now."

"But what was it?" I asked.

"Harmony's disapproval of your attitude toward me, of the desire aroused in you. You will be able to understand it all later."

"What's 'harmony' got to do with it? It's you! It's only that you yourself began to resist."

"And I too did not accept it. It was offensive to me."

I sat up, and pulled my bag over toward me.

"Come on, now! 'She didn't accept me! It was offensive to her...' Oh you women! You just do everything you can to tempt us! You bare your legs, stick out your breasts, walk around in high-heeled shoes. That's very uncomfortable, and yet you do it! You walk and wriggle with all your charm, but as soon as... 'Oh, I don't need that! I'm not that way...' What do you wriggle for then? Hypocrites!

I'm an entrepreneur and I've seen a lot of your sorts. You all want the same thing, only you all act it out differently. So why did you, Anastasia, take off your outer clothes? The weather's not that hot! And then you lolled about on the grass here, with that alluring smile of yours..."

"I am not that comfortable in clothing, Vladimir. I put it on when I leave the woods and go out among people, but only so I can look like everyone else. I just lay down to relax in the sun and not disturb you while you were eating."

"So you didn't want to disturb me... Well, you did!"

"Please forgive me, Vladimir. Of course, you are right about every woman wanting to attract a man's attention, but not just to her legs and breasts. What she wants is not to let pass by the one man who can see more than just those things."

"But nobody's been passing by here! And what is this 'more' that must be seen, when it's your legs that are front and centre? Oh you women, you're so illogical!"

"Yes, unfortunately, that is the way life sometimes turns out... Maybe we should get along, Vladimir! Have you finished eating? Are you rested?"

The thought crossed my mind: is it worth going on with this philosophising wild woman? But I replied:

"Fine, let's go."

3

Beast or Man?

We continued our journey to Anastasia's home, her outer clothes left behind in the tree hollow. Her galoshes too. She was still wearing the short, light-weight frock. She herself picked up my bag and offered to carry it. Barefoot, she walked ahead of me with an amazingly light and graceful step, waving the bag about her with ease.

We talked the whole time. Talking with her on any subject was most interesting. Perhaps because she had her own strange ideas about everything.

Sometimes Anastasia would whirl about while we were walking. She turned her face to me, laughing, and kept on walking backwards for a while, quite absorbed in the conversation without so much as a glance down at her feet. How could she walk like that and not once stumble, or prick her bare feet against the knot of a dry branch? We didn't seem to be following any visible path; on the other hand, our way was not hindered by the tangled undergrowth so common in the taiga.

As she walked she would occasionally touch or quickly brush by a leaf or a twig on a bush. Or, bending over without looking, she would tear off some little blade of grass and... eat it.

"Just like a little creature," I thought.

When berries were handy, Anastasia would offer me a few to eat as we walked. The muscles of her body didn't seem to have any unusual features. Her overall physique appeared quite average. Not too thin and not too plump. A resilient, well-fed and very beautiful body. But, from what I could tell, it possessed a goodly degree of strength and extremely sharp reflexes.

Once when I stumbled and started to fall, my arms outstretched in front of me, Anastasia whirled around with lightning speed, quickly placing her free hand under me, and I landed with my chest on her palm, her fingers spread wide. There she was supporting my body with the palm of one hand, helping it regain its normal position. During all this time she went on talking, with not the slightest sign of strain. After I had straightened up with the help of her hand, we continued on our way, as though nothing whatever had happened. For some reason my mind momentarily rested on the gas pistol I had in my bag.

With all the interesting conversation I hadn't realised how much ground we had actually been covering. All at once Anastasia stopped, put my bag down under a tree and joyfully exclaimed:

"Here we are at home!"

I looked around. A neat little glade, dotted with flowers amidst a host of majestic cedars, but not a single structure to be seen. Not even a hut. In a word, nothing! Not even a primitive lean-to! But Anastasia was beside herself with joy. As though we had arrived at a most comfortable dwelling.

"And where is your house? Where do you eat, sleep, take shelter from the rain?"

"This *is* my house, Vladimir. I have everything here."

A dark sense of disquiet began to come over me.

"Where is everything? Let's have a tea-kettle, so we can at least heat up some water on the fire. Let's have an axe."

"I do not have a kettle or an axe, Vladimir. And it would be best not to light a fire."

"What are you talking about? She doesn't even have a kettle?! The water in my bottle is all gone. You saw when I ate. I even threw the bottle away. Now there's only a couple of swallows of cognac left. To get to the river or the village is a good day's walk, and I'm so tired and thirsty. Where do you get water from? What do you drink out of?"

Seeing my agitation, Anastasia herself showed signs of concern. She quickly took me by the hand and led me through the glade into the forest, admonishing me along the way:

"Not to worry, Vladimir! Please. Don't get upset. I shall take care of everything. You just rest. Get a good sleep. I shall take care of everything. You will not be cold. You are thirsty? I shall give you something to drink right away."

Less than ten or fifteen metres from the glade, beyond a clump of bushes, we came across a small taiga lake. Anastasia quickly scooped up a small quantity of water in her cupped hands and raised it to my face.

"Here is some water. Drink it, please."

"What, are you crazy? How can you drink raw water out of some puddle in the woods? You saw how I was drinking *borzhomi*.[1] On board ship even for washing we pass the river water through a special filter, chlorinate it, ozonise it."

"It is not a puddle, Vladimir. This is pure, living water! Good water! Not half-destroyed water, like yours. You can drink this water, just like mother's milk! Look."

Anastasia raised her cupped hands to her lips and took a drink.

I blurted out:

"Anastasia, are you some kind of beast?"

"Why a beast? Because my bed is not like yours? There are no cars? No appliances?"

"Because you live like a beast, in the forest, you haven't any possessions, and you seem to enjoy that."

"Yes, I enjoy living here."

"There, you see, you just made my point."

"Do you consider, Vladimir, that what distinguishes Man from all other creatures living on Earth is his possession of manufactured objects?"

"Yes! But even more precisely — his civilised existence."

"And do you consider your existence to be more civilised? Yes, of course, you do. But I am not a beast, Vladimir.

"I am Man!"[2]

---

[1] *borzhomi* — a popular kind of mineral water from the Caucasus mountains in Georgia, famous for its health-giving properties.

[2] The word *Man* (with a capital *M*) is used throughout the book to refer to a human being of any gender. For details on the word's usage and the important distinction between *Man* and *human* please see the Translator's Preface.

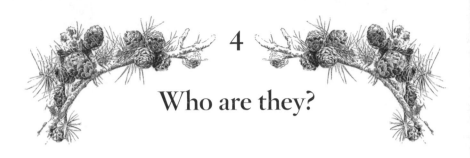

4

Who are they?

Subsequently, after spending three days with Anastasia and observing how this strange young woman lives all by herself in the remote Siberian taiga, I began to understand a little something of her lifestyle, and to be confronted by a number of questions regarding our own.

One of them still haunts me to this day: is our system of education and bringing up children sufficient to comprehend the meaning of existence, to arrange every individual's life-priorities in the correct order? Does it help or hinder our ability to make sense of Man's essence and purpose?

We have set up a vast educational system. It is on the basis of this system that we teach our children and each other — in kindergarten, school, university and post-graduate programmes. It is this system that enables us to invent things, to fly into Space. We structure our lives in accordance with it. Through its help we strive to construct some happiness for ourselves. We strive to fathom the Universe and the atom, along with all sorts of anomalous phenomena. We love to discuss and describe them at great length in sensational stories in both the popular press and scholarly publications.

But there is one phenomenon which, for some reason, we try with all our might to avoid. Desperately try to avoid! One gets the impression that we are afraid to talk about it. We are afraid, I say, because it could so easily knock the wind out of our commonly accepted systems of education and scientific deductions and make a mockery of the objects inherent in our lifestyle! And we try to pretend that such a phenomenon does not exist. But it does! And it will continue to exist, however much we try to turn away from it or avoid it.

Isn't it time to take a closer look at this and, just maybe, through the collective effort of all our human minds together, find an answer to the following question? If you take all our great thinkers, without exception — people who have formulated religious teachings, all sorts of teachings which the vast majority of humanity are following — or at least endeavouring to follow — why is it that, before formulating their teachings, they became recluses, went into solitude — in most cases, to the forest? Not to some super academy, mind you, but to the forest![1]

Why did the Old Testament's Moses go off into a mountain-top forest before returning and presenting to the world the wisdom set forth on his tablets of stone?

Why did Christ Jesus go off, away from his disciples, into the desert, mountains and forest?

Why did a man named Siddhartha Gautama, who lived in India in the sixth century A.D. spend seven years alone in the forest? After which this recluse came out of the forest, back to people, complete with a set of teachings! Teachings which even to this day, many centuries later, arouse a multitude of human minds. And people build huge temples and call these teachings Buddhism. And the man himself eventually came to be known as Buddha.[2]

And what about our own not-so-ancient forebears (now acknowledged as historical figures) — men such as Serafim Sarovsky[3] or Sergiy Radonezhsky?[4] Why did they too go off to become recluses in the

---

[1] Incidentally, even the word *academy*, translated from Greek, means *groves!*

[2] *Buddha* or *Siddhartha Gautama* (623–544 B.C.) — a member of the Imperial Shakya family, who (according to tradition, at least) rejected the wealthy circumstances of his family upbringing and devoted his life to alleviating human suffering. He is occasionally referred to as *Shakyamuni* — 'a recluse (*lit.* departer) from the Shakyas'.

[3] *Serafim Sarovsky (né:* Prokhor Sidorovich Moshnin, 1759–1833) — a monk of the Sarovsky Hermitage near Tambov, who had a gift for healing and foretelling the future. He was particularly concerned about improving the situation of women and in the 1820s helped establish what would become the Holy Trinity Serafimo-Diveevo Women's Monastery. Canonised in 1903, he is now one of the most revered saints of the Russian Orthodox Church.

[4] *Sergiy (né: Varfolomei) Radonezhsky* (1314?–1392) — a monastic reformer from the Rostov area, who devoted his life to the principle of brotherly love and meeting the practical needs of the less fortunate; he also mediated disputes between warring princes. In the 1330s he founded a monastery deep in the Radonezh Forest north of Moscow (now the site of the town of Sergiev Posad, until recently called Zagorsk). He was canonised in 1452.

forest, and how were they able, after a short period of time there, to so fathom the depths of wisdom that the kings of this world made the long journey through uncharted wilderness to seek their advice?

Monasteries and majestic temples were raised at the locations of their respective solitudes. Thus, for example, the Trinity-Sergiev Monastery in the town of Sergiev Posad near Moscow today attracts thousands of visitors each year. And it all started from a single forest recluse.

Why? Who or what enabled these people to obtain their wisdom? Who gave them knowledge, who brought them closer to understanding the essence of life? How did they live, what did they do, what did they think about during their forest solitude?

These questions confronted me some time after my conversations with Anastasia — after I had started reading everything that I could lay my hands on regarding recluses. But even today I haven't found answers. Why has nothing been written about their solitude experiences?

The answers, I think, must be sought through a collective effort. I shall try to describe the events of my three-day stay in the Siberian taiga forest and my impressions from my conversations with Anastasia, in the hopes that someone will be able to fathom the essence of this phenomenon and put together a clearer picture of our way of life.

For now, on the basis of all that I have seen and heard, only one thing is crystal-clear to me: people who live in solitude in the forest, including Anastasia, see what is going on in our lives from a point of view completely different from ours. Some of Anastasia's ideas are the exact opposite of what is commonly accepted. Who is closer to the truth? Who can judge?

My task is simply to record what I have seen and heard, and thereby give others an opportunity to come up with answers.

Anastasia lives in the forest altogether alone. She has no house to call her own, she hardly wears any clothes and does not store any provisions. She is the descendant of people who have been living here for thousands of years and represents what is literally a whole different civilisation. She and those like her have survived to the present day through what I can only term the wisest possible decisions. Very likely the only correct decisions. When they are among us they blend in with us, trying to appear no different from ordinary people, but in their places of habitual residence they merge with Nature. It is not easy to find their habitual dwelling-places. Indeed, Man's presence in such places is betrayed only by the fact that they are more beautiful and better taken care of, like Anastasia's forest glade, for example.

Anastasia was born here and is an integral part of the natural surroundings. In contrast to our celebrated recluses, she did not go off into the forest simply for a time, as they did. She was born in the taiga and visits our world only for brief periods. And on the face of it there seems to be quite a simple explanation for the strong fear that overwhelmed me and made me lose consciousness when I attempted to possess Anastasia — just as we tame a cat, a dog, an elephant, a tiger, an eagle, and so on, here *everything* around has been 'tamed'.[5] And this *everything* is incapable of permitting anything bad to happen to her. Anastasia told me that when she was born and while she was still under a year old, her mother could leave her alone on the grass.

"And you didn't die from hunger?" I asked.

The taiga recluse first looked at me in surprise, but then explained:

"There should be no problems of finding food for Man. One should eat just as one breathes, not paying attention to the food, not distracting one's thought from more important things. The Creator has left that task up to others, so that Man can live as Man, fulfilling his own destiny."

She snapped her fingers, and right away a little squirrel popped up beside her, hopping onto her hand. Anastasia lifted the creature's muzzle up to her mouth, and the squirrel passed from its mouth into hers a cedar nut seed, its shell already removed. This did not seem to me anything out of the ordinary. I remembered how, back at the academic complex near Novosibirsk,[6] a lot of squirrels were quite

[5]*'tamed'* — in this case meaning 'brought into an interrelationship with Man'.

[6]*academic complex* — just outside Novosibirsk there is a whole town known as *Akademgorodok* (lit. 'Academic town') — home of the Siberian branch of the Russian Academy of Sciences as well as Novosibirsk State University — where the professors and researchers live as well as work.

used to people and would beg for food from passers-by, and even get angry if they weren't given anything. Here I was simply observing the process in reverse. But this *here* was the taiga, and I said:

"In the normal world, our world, everything's arranged differently. If you, Anastasia, tried snapping your fingers at a privately-run kiosk,[7] or even beat on a drum, nobody would give you anything, and here you say the Creator has decided everything."

"Who is to blame if Man has decided to change the Creator's creative design? Whether it is for the better or for the worse, that is up to you to divine."

This is the kind of dialogue I had with Anastasia on the question of human sustenance. Her position is simple — it is sinful to waste thought on things like food, and she does not think about it. But for us in our civilised world, as it happens, we are obliged to give it thought.

We know from books, reports in the press and TV programmes, of a multitude of examples of infants who have found themselves out in the wilds and ended up being fed by wolves. Here in the taiga generations of people have made their permanent residence, and their relationship to the animal kingdom is different from ours. I asked Anastasia:

"Why aren't you cold, when here I am in a warm jacket?"

"Because," she replied, "the bodies of people who wrap themselves in clothing to hide from the cold and heat, gradually lose their ability to adapt to changes in their environment. In my case this capacity of the human body has not been lost, and so I have no need of any special clothing."

---

[7]*privately-run kiosk* — small enclosed stands selling food and many other items under private (as opposed to State) control, which began proliferating during the latter days of *perestroika* and are still popular today.

5

A forest bedroom

I wasn't at all equipped to spend a night in the wilds of the forest. Anastasia put me to bed in some kind of cave hollowed out of the ground. Exhausted after my wearying trek, I quickly fell fast asleep. When I woke up, I felt a sense of bliss and comfort, as though I were lying in a magnificently comfortable bed.

The cave, or dugout, was spacious, appointed with small feathery cedar twigs and dried grass which filled the surrounding space with a fragrant aroma. As I stretched and spread my limbs, one hand touched a furry pelt and I determined at once that Anastasia must be something of a hunter. I moved closer to the pelt, pressing my back to its warmth, and decided to have another little snooze.

Anastasia was standing in the entranceway to my forest bedroom. Noticing I was awake, she said at once:

"May this day come to you with blessings, Vladimir. And you should, in turn, greet *it* with your blessing. Only, please, do not be frightened."

Then she clapped her hands, and the 'pelt'... I was horror-struck at the realisation that this was no pelt. Out of the cave a huge bear began to gingerly crawl. Receiving a pat of approval from Anastasia, the bear licked her hand and began lumbering off into the forest. It turned out that she had placed some belladonna herbs under my head for a pillow and made the bear lie down beside me so I wouldn't get cold. She herself had curled up outdoors in front the entranceway.

"Now how could you do such a thing to me, Anastasia? He could have torn me to shreds or crushed me to death!"

"First of all, it is not a *he,* but a *she*-bear. She could not possibly have done anything to harm you," Anastasia responded. "She is very obedient. She really enjoys it when I give her tasks to carry out. She never even budged the whole night — just nuzzled her nose up to my leg and just kept blissfully still, she was so happy. Only she did give a little shudder when you waved your arms about in your sleep and slapped her backside!"

6

Anastasia's morning

Anastasia goes to bed at nightfall in one of the shelters hollowed out by the creatures of the forest, most often in the bear's dugout. When it is warm, she can sleep right on the grass. The first thing she does upon waking is offer an exuberant outburst of joy to the rising Sun, to the new sprouts on all the twigs, to the new shoots of growth popping up from the earth. She touches them with her hands, strokes them, occasionally adjusts something into place. Then she runs over to the little trees and gives them a thump on their trunks. The tree-tops shake and shower down on her something resembling pollen or dew. Then she lies down on the grass and blissfully stretches and squirms. Her whole body becomes covered with what appears to be a moist cream. Then she runs off and jumps into her little lake, splashes about and dives to the bottom. She's a terrific diver!

Her relationship with the animal world around her is very much like people's relationships with their household pets. Many of them watch Anastasia as she does her morning routine. They don't approach her, but all she has to do is look in the direction of one of them and make the tiniest beckoning gesture, and the lucky one jumps up on the spot and rushes to her feet.

I saw how one morning she clowned around, playing with a she-wolf just as one might play with the family dog. Anastasia clapped the wolf on the shoulder and dashed off at full tilt. The wolf gave chase, and just as she was about to catch up with her, Anastasia, still on the run, suddenly jumped in the air, repelled herself with both feet off the trunk of a tree, and dashed off in another direction. The wolf couldn't stop but kept on running past the tree, finally making an about-turn and chasing after the laughing Anastasia.

Anastasia gives absolutely no thought to feeding or clothing herself. She most often walks about nude or semi-nude. She sustains herself with cedar nuts, along with varieties of herbs, berries and mushrooms. She eats only dried mushrooms. She never goes hunting for nuts or mushrooms herself, never stores up any kind of provisions, even for the winter. Everything is prepared for her by the multitude of squirrels dwelling in these parts.

Squirrels storing up nuts for the winter is nothing out of the ordinary — that's what they do everywhere, following their natural instincts. I was struck by something else, though: at the snap of Anastasia's fingers any squirrels nearby would compete to be the first to jump onto her outstretched hand and give her the kernel of an already shelled cedar nut. And whenever Anastasia slaps her leg bent at the knee, the squirrels make some sort of sound, as if signalling the others, and they all start bringing dried mushrooms and other supplies and laying them out before her on the grass. And this they do, it seemed to me, with a good deal of pleasure. I thought she had trained them herself, but Anastasia told me that their actions were instinctive, and the mother squirrel herself teaches this to her little ones by example.

"Perhaps one of my early forebears once trained them, but most likely this is simply what they are destined to do. By the time winter has set in, each squirrel has stored up several times as many supplies as it can use for itself."

To my question "How do you keep from freezing during the winter without the proper clothing?" Anastasia replied with a question of her own: "In your world are there no examples of people able to withstand the cold without special clothing?"

And I remembered the book by Porfiry Ivanov,[1] who went around barefoot and wearing only shorts no matter how cold the weather. It tells in the book how the fascists, wanting to test the endurance abilities of this extraordinary Russian, poured cold water over him in a minus-twenty-degree frost and then made him ride naked on a motorcycle.

---

[1] *Porfiry Korneevich Ivanov* (1899–1983) — a famous proponent of healthy living through closeness to Nature. In his thirties he cured himself of cancer through self-exposure to extremely cold temperatures and spiritual cleansing. After decades of experimentation he formulated a set of twelve ethical and practical principles for health and harmonious relationship with Nature in his popular *Detka* (literally, 'baby'), and gained a substantial following.

In her early childhood, in addition to her mother's milk Anastasia was able to draw upon the milk of many different animals. They freely allowed her access to their nipples. She makes absolutely no ritual of mealtime, never sits down just to eat, but picks berries and sprouts of plants as she walks and continues on with her activities.

By the end of my three-day stay with her I could no longer relate to her as I had done at our first encounter. After all I had seen and heard Anastasia had been transformed for me into some kind of being — but not a beast, since she has such a high degree of intelligence, and then there's her memory! Her memory is such that she, of course, forgets nothing of what she has seen or heard at any moment in time. At times it seemed that her abilities are well beyond the comprehension of the average person. But this very attitude toward her is something that greatly distresses and upsets her.

In contrast to certain people we all know with unusual abilities — people who wrap themselves in an aura of mystery and exclusivity, she constantly tried to explain and reveal the mechanism underlying her abilities, to prove that there was nothing supernatural to Man in them or in her — that she was Man, a woman, and she repeatedly asked me to bear that in mind. I did attempt to keep it in mind after that, and try to find an explanation for this extraordinary phenomenon.

In our civilisation one's brain works to develop a life for one's self, obtain food to eat and satisfy one's sexual instincts. In Anastasia's world no time is spent on these things whatsoever. Even people who find themselves in a situation like the Lykovs'[2] are obliged to constantly give thought to how to feed and shelter themselves. They don't get help from Nature to the same extent as does Anastasia. There are all sorts of tribes living far from civilisation that are not blessed with this kind of contact. According to Anastasia, it is because their thoughts are not pure enough. Nature and the animal world feel this.

[2]See footnote 3 in Chapter 2: "Encounter".

7

Anastasia's ray

I think the most unusual, mystical phenomenon I witnessed during my time in the forest was Anastasia's ability to see not only individuals at great distance but also what was going on in their lives. Possibly other recluses have had a similar ability.

She did this with the help of an invisible ray. She maintained this was something everybody has, but people don't know about it and are unable to make use of it.

"Man has still not invented anything that is not already in Nature. The technology behind television is but a poor imitation of the possibilities of this ray."

The ray being invisible, I didn't believe in it, in spite of her repeated attempts to demonstrate and explain how it worked, to find some proof or plausible explanation. And then one day...

"Tell me, Vladimir, what do you think daydreams are? And do many people dream of the future?"

"Daydreaming? I think a lot of people are able to do that. It's when you imagine yourself in a future of your own desire."

"Fine. So, you do not deny that Man has the capacity to visualise his own future, to visualise various specific situations?"

"That I don't deny."

"And what about intuition?"

"Intuition... It's probably the feeling one has when, instead of analysing what or why something might happen, some sort of feelings suggest the right thing to do."

"So, you do not deny that in Man there exists something besides ordinary analytical reasoning that helps him determine his own and others' behaviour?"

"Well, let's say that's true."

"Wonderful! Good!" exclaimed Anastasia. "Now, the night-dream. The night-dream — what is that? The dreams almost all people have when they are asleep."

"The night dream — that's... I really don't know what that is. When you're asleep, a dream is simply a dream."

"All right, all right. Let us call it just a dream. But you do not deny it exists? You and other people are aware that someone in a dream state, when his body is almost beyond the control of a part of his consciousness, can see people and all sorts of things going on."

"Well that, I think, is something nobody will deny."

"But still in a dream people can communicate, hold conversations, empathise?"

"Yes, they can."

"And what do you think, can a person control his dream? Call up in the dream images and events he would like to see? Just like on ordinary television, for example."

"I don't think that would work out for anyone. The dream, somehow, comes all by itself."

"You are wrong. Man can control everything. Man is designed to control everything.

"The ray I am telling you about consists of information one possesses — concepts, intuitions, emotional feelings and, as a result, of dream-like visions consciously controlled by Man's will."

"How can a dream be controlled in a dream?"

"Not in a dream. Wide awake! As if pre-programmed, and with absolute accuracy. You only experience this in a dream and it is chaotic. Man has lost most of his ability to control, to control natural phenomena and himself. So he has decided that a night-dream is simply an incidental by-product of his tired brain. In fact, almost everybody on the Earth... Well, maybe I should try helping you see something at a distance right here and now?"

"Go ahead."

"Lie down on the grass and relax, let go, so that your body draws less energy. It is important that you are comfortable. Nothing in the way? Now think about the person you know best — your wife, for example. Recollect her habits, how she walks, her clothing, where you think she might be right now, and turn the whole thing over to your imagination."

I remembered my wife, knowing that at that moment she might be at our country home. I imagined the house and some of the furnishings and things. I remembered a great deal, and in some detail, but I didn't see anything. I told Anastasia about all this, and she replied:

"You are not able to let go all the way, as though you were going to go to sleep. I shall help you. Close your eyes. Stretch out your arms in different directions."

Closing my eyes, I felt her fingers touch mine. I began to immerse myself in a dream, or a wakeful doze...

...There was my wife standing in the kitchen of our country home. Over her usual dressing gown she was wearing a knitted cardigan. That meant it was cool in the house. Again some kind of trouble with the heating system.

My wife was making coffee on the gas stove. And something else, in the small crock-pot. My wife's face was gloomy and unhappy. Her movements were sluggish. All at once she turned her head, tripped over to the window, looked out at the rain and smiled. The coffee on the stove was spilling over. She picked up the pot with its overflowing liquid but didn't frown or get upset as she usually did. She took off the cardigan...

I woke up.

"Well? Did you see anything?" asked Anastasia.

"I did indeed. But maybe it was just an ordinary dream?"

"How could it be ordinary? Did you not *plan* on seeing your wife in particular?"

"Yes, I did. And I saw her. But where is the proof that she was actually there in the kitchen at the moment I saw her in the dream?"

"Remember this day and hour, Vladimir, if you want to have proof. When you get home, ask her. Was there not something else out of the ordinary that you noticed?"

"Can't think of anything."

"You mean to say you did not notice a smile on your wife's face when she went over to the window? She was smiling, and she did not get upset when the coffee spilled."

"That I did notice. She probably saw something interesting out the window which made her feel good."

"All she saw out the window was rain. Rain which she never likes."

"So, why was she smiling?"

"I too was watching your wife through my ray and warmed her up."

"So, *your* ray warmed her up — what about mine? Too cold?"

"You were only looking out of curiosity, you did not put any feeling into it."

"So, your ray can warm people up at a distance?"

"Yes, it can do that."

"And what else can it do?"

"Obtain certain kinds of information, or transmit. It can cheer up a person's mood and partially take away someone's illness. There are a lot of other things it can do, depending on the energy available and the degree of feeling, will and desire."

"And can you see the future?"

"Of course."

"The past too?"

"The future and the past — they are pretty much the same thing. It is only the external details that are different. The essence always remains unchanged."

"How can that be? What can remain unchanged?"

"Well, for example, a thousand years ago people wore different clothes. They had different instruments at their disposal. But that is not the essence. Back a thousand years ago, just like today, people had the same feelings. Feelings are not subject to time.

"Fear, joy, love. Just think, Yaroslav the Wise,[1] Ivan the Terrible[2] and the Egyptian pharaohs were all capable of loving a woman with exactly the same feelings as you or any other man today."

"Interesting. Only I'm not sure what it means. You say every person can have a ray like this?"

"Of course everyone can. Even today people still have feelings and intuitions, the capacity to dream of the future, to conjecture, to

---

[1] *Yaroslav the Wise* (Russian: *Yaroslav Mudry*; 978?–1054) — a Grand Prince of Kiev who managed to impose a degree of unity on the warring princes of what was then Kievan Russia, consolidate its southern and western borders and establish dynastic liaisons with a number of European nations.

[2] *Ivan the Terrible* (Russian: *Ivan IV, Ivan Grozny*, 1530–1584) — the first Russian Grand Prince to proclaim himself *Tsar of all the Russias*. His reign was marked by bloody repression of political rivals and wealthy aristocrats, stronger ties with England, political and social reforms at home and an expansion of the Russian Empire eastward.

visualise specific situations, to have dreams while they sleep — only it is all chaotic and uncontrollable."

"Maybe some kind of training's necessary. Some exercises could be developed?"

"Some exercises might help. But you know, Vladimir, there is one absolute condition before the ray can be controlled by the will..."

"And what condition is that?"

"It is absolutely necessary to keep one's thoughts pure, as the strength of the ray depends on the strength of radiant feelings."

"Now there you go! Just when everything was starting to get clear... What have pure thoughts got to do with it? 'Radiant feelings'?"

"They are what power the ray."

"That's enough, Anastasia! I'm already losing interest. Next you'll be adding something else."

"I have already told you what is essential."

"You can say what you like, but you've got too many darn conditions! Let's talk about something else. Something a little simpler..."

All day long Anastasia engages in meditation, visualising all sorts of situations from our past, present and future life.

Anastasia possesses a phenomenal memory. She can remember a multitude of people she has seen in her imagination or through her ray, and what they have been going through mentally. She's a consummate actress — she can imitate the way they walk and talk, and even think the way they do. She concentrates her thought on the life experience of millions of people in the past and present. She uses the knowledge she gains from this to visualise the future and to help others. This she does at a great distance by means of her invisible ray, and the ones she helps through suggestion or decision, or the ones she heals, haven't the slightest idea that she is helping them.

It was only later that I found out that similar rays invisible to the eye, only of different degrees of strength, emanate from every individual.

The academician Anatoly Akimov[3] photographed them with special devices and published his results in 1996 in the May issue of the magazine *Chudesa i prikliuchenia (Wonders and Adventures)*. Unfortunately, we are unable to use these rays as she does. In scientific literature a phenomenon such as this ray is known as a *torsion field*.

Anastasia's world-view is unusual and interesting.

"What is God, Anastasia? Does He exist? If so, why hasn't anyone seen Him?"

"God is the interplanetary Mind, or Intelligence. He is not to be found in a single mass. Half of Him is in the non-material realm of the Universe. This is the sum total of all energies. The other half of Him is dispersed across the Earth, in every individual, in every Man. The dark forces strive to block these particles."

"What do you think awaits our civilisation?"

"In the long term, a realisation of the futility of the technocratic path of development and a movement back to our primal origins."

"You mean to say that all our scholars are immature beings who are leading us into a dead end?"

"I mean to say that they are accelerating the process, they are bringing you closer to the realisation that you are on the wrong path."

"And so? All the cars and houses we build are pointless?"

"Yes."

"You're not bored living here alone, Anastasia? Alone, without television or telephone?"

"These primitive things you mention, Man has possessed them right from the very beginning, only in a more perfect form. I have them."

---

[3] *Anatoly Evgenevich Akimov* — Director of the International Institute of Theoretical and Applied Physics of the Russian Academy of Natural Sciences.

"Both television and telephone?"

"Well, what is television? A device through which certain information is served up to an almost atrophied human imagination and scenes and story-plots are acted out. I can, through my own imagination, outline the plot of any story, and act out the most improbable situations — even take part in them myself, just like having an influence on the outcome. ...Oh dear, I suppose I have not been making myself too clear, eh?"

"And the telephone?"

"Every Man can talk with any other individual without the aid of a telephone. All that is needed is the will and desire of both parties and a developed imagination."

8

Concert in the taiga

I proposed that she herself come to Moscow and appear on TV.

"Just think, Anastasia, with your beauty you could easily be a world-class fashion or photomagazine model!"

And at this point I realised that she was no stranger to earthly matters — like all women, she delighted in being a beauty. Anastasia burst out laughing.

"A world-class beauty, eh?" She echoed my question and then, like a child, began to frolic about, prancing through the glade like a model on a catwalk.

I was amused at her imitation of a fashion model, placing one foot in front of the other in turn as she walked, showing off imaginary outfits. Finding myself getting into the act, I applauded and announced:

"And now, ladies and gentlemen, your attention, please! Performing before you will be that magnificent gymnast, second-to-none, that incomparable beauty: Anastasia!"

This announcement tickled her fancy even more. She ran out into the middle of the glade and executed an incredible flying somersault — first forward, then backward, then to the side, both left and right, then an amazingly high leap into the air. Grasping a tree-branch with one hand, she swung herself around it twice before flinging her body over to another tree. After yet another somersault, she began to bow coquettishly to my applause. Then she ran off out of the glade and hid behind some thick bushes. Anastasia peeped smilingly out from behind them, as though they were a theatre-curtain, impatiently awaiting my next announcement.

I remembered a videotape I had of some of my favourite songs being performed by popular artists. I would watch it occasionally in the evening in my cabin aboard ship. I had this tape in mind (but not with the thought that Anastasia would actually be able to reproduce anything from it) as I announced:

"Ladies and gentlemen, I now present to you the star singers of our current stage, in a performance of their top hits. Your attention, please!"

Oh, how wrong I had been in my estimate of her abilities. What happened next I could not possibly have predicted. No sooner had Anastasia made her entrance from behind her improvised curtain, than she launched into the authentic voice of Alla Pugachova.[1] No, it wasn't just a parody or an imitation, but Alla herself, effortlessly conveying not only her voice, but her intonations and emotions as well.

But an even more amazing feature was to come. Anastasia accentuated particular words, adding something of her own, infusing the song with her own supplemental attenuations, so that Alla Pugachova's own performance, which before, it seemed, nobody else could even begin to surpass, now called forth a whole new range of additional feelings, illuminating the images even more clearly.

In a magnificently executed overall performance of the song:

Once lived an artist alone,
Canvases all through his home.
He loved an actress, he thought,
Flowers were her love, fresh-grown.
He went and sold his big home,
Sold every canvas he owned,
And with the money he bought
Whole fields of flowers, fresh-grown.

Anastasia put particular emphasis on the word "canvas".

She screamed out this word in fright and surprise. A canvas is an artist's most prized possession — without it he can no longer

[1] *Alla Borisovna Pugachova* (also spelt: *Pugacheva*, 1949–) — one of the most popular Russian stage and screen singers of the twentieth century, the recipient of a number of national and international awards. Pugachova, known as a 'national Russian legend', has toured extensively abroad, including Canada and America. Her *Alla* entertainment company grew out of *Alla Pugachova's Theatre of Song*, which she has headed as Artistic Director since 1988.

create — and here he is giving up the most precious thing he owns for the sake of his loved one. Later, as she sang the words *Then she went off on the train,* Anastasia tenderly portrayed the artist in love, looking longingly after the departing train which was carrying off his loved one forever. She portrayed his pain, his despair, his perplexed state of mind.

I was too shaken by everything I had seen and heard to applaud at the end of the song. Anastasia bowed, anticipating the applause and, hearing none, launched into a new song with even more enthusiasm. She performed all of my favourite songs, in the same order they had been recorded on the videotape. And every single song, which I had heard so many times before, was now even clearer and more meaningful in her rendition.

Upon completing the last song on the tape, still hearing no applause, Anastasia retreated 'backstage'. Too dumbfounded to speak, I remained seated in silence, still feeling an extraordinary impression from what I had just witnessed. Then I jumped up, began applauding and cried:

"Terrific, Anastasia! Encore! Bravo! All performers on stage!"

Anastasia gingerly stepped forth and gave a bow. I kept on shouting:

"Encore! Bravo!" — clapping my hands and stamping my feet.

She too livened up. She clapped her hands and cried:

"*Encore* — does that mean 'Again'?"

"Yes, again! And again! And again!... You did it so marvellously, Anastasia! Better than the singers themselves! Even better than our top stars!"

I fell silent and began attentively studying Anastasia. I thought how multifaceted her soul must be if she could infuse her singing performance with so many new, splendid, clear features. She too stood motionless, silently and enquiringly looking at me.

"Anastasia, do you have any song of your own? Couldn't you sing something of your own, something I haven't heard before?"

"I could, but my song does not have any words. Would you still like to hear it?"

"Please sing your song."

"Fine."

And she started in singing her most unusual song. Anastasia first screamed like a newborn baby. Then her voice started sounding quiet, tender and caressing. She stood beneath a tree, her hands clasped to her breast, her head bowed. It was like a lullaby, gently caressing a little one with her voice. Her voice spoke to him of something very tender. Her soft voice, amazingly pure, caused everything around to grow silent — the birds' singing, the chirping of the crickets in the grass. At that point Anastasia seemed to take absolute delight in the little one waking from sleep. The sound of rejoicing could be heard in her voice. The incredibly high-pitched sounds soared above the Earth before taking flight into the heights of infinity. Anastasia's voice first pleaded, then went into battle, and once again caressed the little one and bestowed joy upon all around.

I too felt this all-pervading sense of joy. And when she finished her song, I joyfully exclaimed:

"And now, my dear ladies and gentlemen, a unique and never-to-be-repeated number by the top animal trainer in the world! The most agile, brave, charming trainer, capable of taming any beast of prey on Earth! Behold and tremble!"

Anastasia positively squealed with delight, leapt into the air, clapped her hands in rhythm, shouted something, started in whistling. Something I could never have imagined began taking place in the glade.

First the she-wolf made her entrance. She leapt out of the bushes and stopped at the edge of the glade, giving a puzzled look around. In the trees furthest from the glade squirrels sprang from branch to branch. Two eagles circled low overhead, while little creatures of some kind rustled in the bushes. With the sharp crackle of dry twigs as he broke and crushed the bushes, a huge bear lumbered out into the glade and stopped, as though embedded in the ground, just short of Anastasia. The wolf began growling at him disapprovingly, since the bear had approached so close to Anastasia without an invitation.

Anastasia ran up to the bear, playfully stroking his muzzle, then grabbed him by his front paws and stood him upright. Judging by the fact that she didn't seem to be exerting much physical effort in this, the bear himself must have been carrying out her commands according to how much he understood and how he interpreted them.

He stood stock still, trying to understand what was desired of him. Anastasia took a running leap and, grabbing hold of the thick scruff of the bear's neck, did a handstand on his shoulders, jumping off again with a somersault on her way down. Then she took the bear by one paw and started to bend over, pulling the bear after her — creating the impression that she was tossing him over her shoulder. This trick would have been impossible if the bear had not been able to do it himself. Anastasia simply guided him. It looked at first as though the bear was going to fall on Anastasia, but at the last moment he reached out a paw to the ground and broke his fall. He was no doubt doing everything he could not to harm his mistress or friend. In the meantime the wolf was become more and more concerned — she was already standing at the place of the action, thrashing from side to side, growling or howling with displeasure.

At the edge of the glade there appeared several more wolves, and when Anastasia was on the point of yet another routine 'toss' of the bear over her shoulder, the bear, attempting to do the trick properly, fell over on his side and remained motionless.

At last the wolf, now at her wits' end, and with a malicious grin, made a leap in the bear's direction. With lightning speed Anastasia placed herself in the wolf's path. The wolf braked with all fours, somersaulted over her back, bumping into Anastasia's leg. Immediately Anastasia put one hand on the back of the wolf, who obediently crouched to the ground. With her other hand she began waving, as she had done that first time with me when I had tried to embrace her without her consent.

The forest around us began to make a rustling sound — not threateningly, but with some agitation. The agitation was felt as well in all the big and little creatures jumping, running and hiding. Anastasia began taking away the agitation. First, she stroked the wolf, slapped her on the back and sent her off out of the glade as though she were a pet dog. The bear was still lying on his side in an uncomfortable pose, like a fallen scarecrow. He was probably waiting to see what else was required of him. Anastasia went over to him, made him stand up, stroked his muzzle and sent him out of the glade like the wolf.

Anastasia, blushing and cheerful, ran over and sat down beside me, breathed in deeply and slowly exhaled. I noticed that her breathing all at once became even, as though she hadn't been carrying out any extraordinary exercises at all.

"They do not understand play-acting, and they ought not to — it is not entirely a good thing," Anastasia remarked. Then she asked me: "Well, how was I? Do you think I could find any kind of work in your life?"

"You're terrific, Anastasia, but we already have all that, and our circus trainers show us a lot of interesting tricks with animals, but you don't have a hope of breaking through all the red tape to even get started. There are so many formalities and machinations to deal with. You don't have any experience in that."

The remainder of our play consisted in going over possible alternatives: where could Anastasia get a job in our world and how would she overcome the formalities in the way? But no easy alternative presented itself, since Anastasia had neither a residence permit nor proof of education, and nobody would believe the stories about her origins on the basis of her abilities, no matter how extraordinary they might be. Suddenly turning serious, Anastasia said:

"Of course I would like to visit one of the big cities again, maybe Moscow, to see how accurate I was in visualising certain situations from your life. For one thing, I am at a complete loss to understand how the dark forces manage to fool women to such a degree that they unwittingly attract men with the charms of their bodies, and thereby deprive them of the opportunity of making a real choice — to choose someone close to their heart. And then they themselves suffer for not being able to create a real family, since..."

And once again she launched into deep and poignant discussions about sex, family and the upbringing of children, and I could only think: "The most incredible thing in all I have seen and heard is her ability to talk about our lifestyle and understand it in such specific detail!"

9

Who lights a new star?

On the second night, fearing that Anastasia would once again assign me her she-bear or concoct up some new device to keep me warm, I categorically refused to go to sleep at all unless she herself lay down beside me. I thought that as long as she was beside me she wouldn't be up to any tricks. And I told her:

"You've invited me as a guest, I take it. In your home. I imagined there would be at least a few buildings here, but you won't even let me light a fire, and you offer me a beastie to keep me company at night. If you don't have a normal home, what's the point of inviting a guest?"

"All right, Vladimir. Do not worry, please, do not be afraid. Nothing bad is going to happen to you. If you want, I shall lie down beside you and keep you warm."

This time in the dugout cave there were even more cedar branches strewn around, along with neatly arranged dry grasses, and there were also branches stuck on the wall.

I got undressed. I put my sweater and trousers under my head for a pillow. I lay down and covered myself with my jacket. The cedar twigs gave off that same bacteria-killing aroma described in the popular literature as capable of purifying the air. Though here in the taiga the air is already so pure, the air in the cave was particularly easy to breathe. The dried grasses and flowers contributed a still more unusual delicate fragrance.

Anastasia kept her word and lay down beside me. I sensed the fragrance of her body, which surpassed all other odours. It was more pleasant than the most delicate perfume I had ever sensed from a woman's body. But now I had no thought of wanting to possess her. After my attempt to do so on the way to the glade, which had resulted at the time in an attack of fear and loss of consciousness, I no longer felt aroused by fleshly desires, even when I saw her naked.

I lay down and dreamt of the son my wife never bore to me. And I thought: Wouldn't it be wonderful if my son could be borne by Anastasia! She is so healthy, sturdy and beautiful! The child, then, too would be healthy. He would look like me. Like her too, but more like me. He would be a strong and clever individual. He would know a lot. He would become talented and prosper.

I imagined our infant son sucking at his mother's nipple and involuntarily put my hand on Anastasia's warm, supple breast. Immediately a shiver ran through my whole body and then dissipated at once, but it wasn't a shiver of fear, but something else, extraordinarily pleasing. I didn't take my hand away, but only held my breath and waited for what might happen. Next thing I noticed was the feeling of the soft palm of her hand on mine. She did not push me away.

I raised my head and began looking into Anastasia's marvellous face. The white twilight of the northern night made it seem even more attractive. I couldn't take my gaze off her. Her greyish-blue eyes looked at me tenderly. I didn't restrain myself, but bent closer and, quickly and carefully, with just the slightest touch, planted a kiss on her half-open lips. Once more a pleasing shiver ran through my body. My face was enshrouded with the fragrance of her breath. Her lips didn't utter, as the last time, "Do not do this!... Calm down!", and I had no fear at all. I was still haunted by the prospect of a son. And when Anastasia tenderly embraced me, stroked my hair and gave her whole body to me, I felt something indescribable!

Only upon awaking in the morning was I able to realise that this kind of magnificent feeling, blissful excitement and satisfaction was something I had never once experienced in my entire life. Another peculiar thing: after a night spent with a woman I had always felt a sense of physical fatigue, but here everything was different. In addition, I had the feeling of some kind of great co-creation. My satisfaction wasn't just something physical, but had another dimension I couldn't quite comprehend, one I had never experienced before, extraordinarily lovely and joyful. The thought even flashed through my mind that life was worth living just for this feeling alone. And why had I never experienced anything that even came close to this before, even though there had been all sorts of women — beautiful women, beloved women, women experienced in love?

Anastasia was a girl. A tender, quivering girl. But beyond that there was something in her that belonged not to a single woman I had known. What was it?

And where had she gone now? I made my way over to the entrance of the cozy dug-out cave, poked my head out and looked out into the glade.

The glade was situated at a slightly lower level than my night-time resting-place. It was covered by a layer of morning mist a half-metre thick. In this mist I could see Anastasia spinning around with outstretched arms. A little cloud of mist was forming about her. And when it covered her completely, Anastasia sprang easily into the air, stretched out her legs in a split just like a ballerina, flew over the layer of mist, landed in a different spot and once more, laughing, spun a new cloud around her, through which could be seen the rays of the rising Sun, gently caressing her body. It was a charming and delightful scene, and I cried out with an overflow of emotion:

"Ana-sta-SI-ya![1] Good morning, my splendid forest fairy, Antastasi-ya-ya!"

"Good morning, Vladimir!" she joyfully called out in response.

"It's so delightful, so wonderful out right now! Why is that?" I cried as loud as I could.

Anastasia lifted up her hands toward the Sun, and began laughing with that happy, alluring laugh of hers, calling out to me (and someone else besides, high above) in a sing-song voice:

"Out of all the creatures in the Universe only Man is given an experience like that!

"Only men and women sincerely desiring to have a child between them!

"Only Man having such an experience lights a new star in the heavens!

"Only Ma-a-an striving for creation and co-creation!

"Tha-ank yo-o-u!" And, addressing me alone, she quickly added: "Only Man striving for creation and co-creation, and not for satisfaction of his carnal needs."

---

[1]*Ana-sta-SI-ya* — As noted in the Translator's Preface, this reflects the Russian pronunciation of her name, with the stress on the syllable *SI* (pronounced 'see').

And again she went off in trills of laughter, leapt high into the air, stretched her legs into a split as though soaring over the mist. Then she came running over, sat down beside me at the entrance to our night-time resting-place and began combing her golden tresses with her fingers, lifting them up from the bottom.

"So, you don't consider sex to be something sinful?" I asked.

Anastasia fell silent. She looked at me in amazement and responded:

"Was *that* the same kind of 'sex' the word implies in your world? And if not, then what is more sinful — to give of yourself so that a Man can come into the world, or to hold back and not allow a Man to be born? A real Man!"

I started thinking. In actual fact, my night-time closeness with Anastasia could not possibly be described by our usual word 'sex'. Then what *did* happen last night? What term *would* be appropriate here? Again I asked:

"And why did anything even approaching that experience never happen with me before — or, for that matter, I would venture to say, with hardly anybody else in the world?"

"You see, Vladimir, the dark forces are constantly trying to make Man give into base fleshly passions, to stop him from experiencing God-given grace. They try all sorts of tricks to persuade people that satisfaction is something you can easily obtain, thinking only of carnal desire. And at the same time they separate Man from truth. The poor deceived women who are ignorant of this spend their lives accepting nothing but suffering and searching for the grace they have lost. But they are searching for it in the wrong places. No woman can restrain a man from fornication if she allows herself to submit to him merely to satisfy his carnal needs. If that has happened, their marital life will not be a happy one.

"Their marital life is only an illusion of togetherness, a lie, a deception accepted by convention. For the woman immediately becomes a fornicator, regardless of whether she is married to the man or not.

"Oh, how many laws and conventions mankind has invented in an attempt to artificially strengthen this false union! Laws both religious and secular. All in vain. All they have done is caused people to play around, accommodate themselves and imagine that such a union exists. One's innermost thoughts invariably remain unchanged, subject to nobody and nothing.

"Christ Jesus saw this. And trying to counteract it, he said: 'Anyone who looks at a woman lustfully has already committed adultery with her in his heart.'[2]

"Then you, in your not-so-distant past have tried to attach shame to anyone who leaves his family. But nothing, at any time or in any situation, has been able to stop Man's desire to seek out that sense of intuitively felt grace — the greatest satisfaction. And to persist in seeking it.

"A false union is a frightening thing.

"Children! Do you see, Vladimir? Children! They sense the artificiality, the falsity of such a union. And this makes them sceptical about everything their parents tell them. Children sub-consciously sense the lie even during their conception. And that has a bad effect on them.

"Tell me who — what individual — would want to come into the world as a result of carnal pleasures alone? We would all like to be created under a great impulsion of love, the aspiration to creation itself, and not simply come into the world as a result of someone's carnal pleasure.

"People who have come into a false union will then look for true satisfaction in secret, apart from each other. They will strive to possess body after body, or make paltry and fateful use of their own bodies, realising only intuitively that they are drifting farther and farther away from the true happiness of a true union."

"Anastasia, wait!", I said. "Can it be that men and women are doomed this way if the first time all that happens between them is sex? Is there no turning back, no possibility of correcting the situation?"

"There is. I now know what to do. But where do I find the right words to express it? I am always looking for them — the right words. I have been looking for them in the past and in the future. But I have not found them. Perhaps they are right in front of me, after all? And

---

[2] Matth. 5: 28 (*New International Version*).

then they will appear, new words will be born — words capable of reaching people's hearts and minds. New words for the ancient truth about their primal origins."

"Don't panic, Anastasia! Use existing words to start with, just as an approximation... What else is needed for true satisfaction, apart from two bodies?"

"Complete awareness! A mutual striving to create. Sincerity and purity of motive."

"How do you know all this, Anastasia?"

"I am not the only one who knows about it. A number of enlightened people have tried to explain it to the world — Veles, Krishna, Rama, Shiva,[3] Christ, Mohammed, Buddha."

"You've what... read about all these people? Where? When?"

"I have not read about them, I simply know what they said, what they thought about, what they wanted to accomplish."

"So sex by itself, according to you, is bad?"

"Very bad. It leads Man away from truth, destroys families. An enormous amount of energy is wasted."

"Then why do so many different magazines publish pictures of naked women in erotic poses, why are there so many films with erotica and sex? And all of this is extremely popular. Demand generates supply. So, you're trying to say that our humanity is completely bad?"

"Humanity is not bad, but the devices of the dark forces obscuring spirituality by provoking base carnal desires — these are very powerful devices. They bring people a lot of grief and suffering. They act through women, exploiting their beauty. A beauty whose real purpose is to engender and support in men the spirit of the poet, the artist, the creator. But to do that women themselves must be pure. If there is not sufficient purity, they start trying to attract men by

[3]*Veles* — in the Russian-Slavic tradition: the god of wisdom and Nature, one of the *Triglav* (Trinity) and the incarnation of God the Creator *Rod* on earth. *Krishna* — an earthly incarnation of god Vishnu, one of the *Trimurti* (the three personalities of God in the Hindu tradition), responsible for the maintenance of the world. *Rama* — a god-king and an earthly incarnation of Vishnu (in the Hindu tradition). *Shiva* — one of the *Trimurti* along with Vishnu and Brahma. While Brahma is seen as the creator the world, Shiva is held to be responsible for destroying it at the end of each cosmic cycle.

fleshly charms. The outward beauty of empty vessels. In the upshot, the men are deceived and the women must suffer their whole lives on account of this deception."

"So what, then, is the result?" I queried. "Through all the millennia of their existence, mankind has not been able to overcome these devices of the dark forces? That would mean they are stronger than Man. Man hasn't been able to overcome them, in spite of the appeals by spiritually enlightened people, as you put it? So, is it downright impossible to overcome them? Or maybe it's not necessary?"

"It *is* necessary. Absolutely necessary!"

"Who then can do it?"

"Women! Women who have been able to grasp the truth and their own appointed purpose. Then the men will change too."

"Oh, no, Anastasia, I doubt it. A normal man will always be aroused by a pretty woman's legs, her breasts... Especially when you're on a business trip or on holiday far away from your partner. That's the way things are. And nobody here will change anything, they won't do it any other way."

"But I did it with you."

"What did you do?"

"Now you are no longer able to indulge in that harmful sex."

All at once a terrible thought hit me like a flood, and started chasing away the magnificent feeling that had been born in me during the night.

"What have you done, Anastasia? What? I'm now... what — I'm now... impotent?"

"On the contrary, you have now become a real man. Only the usual sex will be repugnant to you. It does not bring what you experienced last night, and what you experienced last night is possible only when you desire to have a child and the woman wants the same from you. When she loves you."

"Loves? But under those conditions... That can happen only a few times during one's whole life!"

"I assure you, Vladimir, that is enough for your whole life to be happy. You will feel the same way eventually... People enter many times afresh into sexual interaction only through the flesh — not realising that true satisfaction in the flesh is impossible to attain. A man and a woman who unite on every plane of existence, impelled by radiant inspiration, earnestly aspiring to the act of creation, experience tremendous satisfaction. The Creator gave this experience to Man alone. No transitory thing, this satisfaction, no! It never can compare with fleeting, fleshly gratification. As you cherish the feelings from it over time, all planes of being will, with influence sublime, happify your life and the woman too — a woman who can give birth to a creation in the Creator's own image and likeness, His design!"

Anastasia held out her hand toward me, trying to move closer. I quickly darted away from her into a corner of the cave and cried:

"Out of my way!"

She got up. I crawled outside and backed off from her a few steps.

"You have deprived me, quite possibly, of my chief pleasure in life! Everybody strives for it, everybody thinks about it, only they don't talk about it out loud."

"They are illusions, Vladimir, these pleasures of yours. I have helped save you from a terrible, harmful and sinful appetite."

"Illusion or not — doesn't make any difference. It's a pleasure recognised by everyone! Don't even think of trying to save me from any other 'harmful' appetites, as you see them. Or by the time I get out of here I'll be... — no relations with women, no drinks or appetizers, no smoking! That's not something most people are used to in normal life."

"Well, what good is there in drinking, smoking, senseless and harmful digestion of such a huge quantity of animal meat, when there are so many splendid plants created especially for Man's nourishment?"

"You go and feed yourself with plants, if you like. But don't come near me. A lot of us get pleasure out of smoking, drinking, sitting down to a good meal. That's how we do things, do you understand? That's how!"

"But everything you name is bad and harmful."

"Bad? Harmful? If guests come to celebrate at my place, and they sit down at the table and I tell them: 'Here are some nuts to gnaw on, have an apple, drink water and don't smoke' — now *that* would be bad."

"Is that the most important thing, when you get together with friends — to sit right down at the table and drink, eat and smoke?"

"Whether it's the most important thing or not is beside the point. That's how people behave all over the world. Some countries even have ritual dishes — roast turkey, for example."

"That is not accepted by everyone even in your world."

"Maybe not by everyone, but I happen to live among normal people."

"Why do you consider the people around you to be the most normal?"

"Because they're in the majority."

"That is not a good enough argument."

"It's not good enough for you, because it's something impossible to explain to you."

My anger at Anastasia began to pass. I recalled hearing about medical prescriptions and sex therapists and the thought came to me that if she *had* somehow injured me, the doctors would be able to fix it. I said:

"Okay, Anastasia. Let's make peace. I'm no longer angry at you. I thank you for the wonderful night. Only don't you try saving me from any more of my habits. As far as sex goes, I'll fix the situation with the help of our doctors and modern medicines. Let's go for a swim."

I began heading for the lake, admiring the morning woods. Just as my good mood was beginning to come back, she— well, there you go again! Walking behind me, she piped up:

"Medicines and doctors will not help you now. To put everything back the way it was, they will have to erase your memory of everything that happened and everything you felt."

Stunned, I stopped in my tracks.

"Then you put everything back the way it was."

"I cannot."

Again I was overwhelmed by a feeling of rampant rage — and, at the same time, fear.

"You! You brazen—! You poke your nose in where it doesn't belong and turn my life upside down! So, you played a nasty trick on me! And now you say you can't fix it?"

"I did not play any nasty tricks. After all, you wanted a son so badly. But so many years had gone by, and you still did not have a son. And none of the women in your life would bear you a son. I also wanted a child by you, a son too. And that is something I can do...

"And why are you getting so concerned ahead of time that things are going to go badly for you? Maybe you'll still come to understand.

"Please do not be afraid of me, Vladimir, I am certainly not trying to meddle with your mind. This happened all on its own. You got what you wanted.

"And I would still very much like to save you from at least one mortal sin."

"And what's that?"

"Pride."

"You're a funny one. Your philosophy and lifestyle aren't human."

"What do you find in me so inhuman that it frightens you?"

"You live all alone in the forest, and communicate with plants and animals. Nobody in our society even comes close to that kind of life."

"How can that be, Vladimir? Why?" Anastasia exclaimed, flustered. "Your *dachniks*[4] — they too communicate with plants and animals, only not consciously. But they will understand one day. Many have already begun to understand."

"Oh, come on! Now she's a *dachnik?* And this ray of yours. You know a lot, but you don't read books. You must be some kind of mystic!"

"I shall try to explain everything to you, Vladimir. Only not all at once. I am trying, but I cannot find the right words. Comprehensible words. Please believe me. All my abilities are inherent in Man. It is something Man was given right from the start. Back in the days of his primal origins. And everyone could do the same today. Nevertheless, people are starting to go back to their primal origins. It will be a gradual process after the forces of light triumph!

"What about your 'concert'? You sang in all sorts of different voices, you portrayed my favourite artists, and even in the same order as on my videotape."

---

[4]*dachniks* — people who spend time (their days off, especially summer holidays) tending a garden at their *dacha,* or cottage in the country. See further details in the Translator's Preface and the Editor's Afterword.

"That is right, Vladimir. You know, I once saw that tape of yours. I shall tell you later how it happened."

"And what — you... right off memorised the words and tunes of all the songs?"

"Yes, I memorised them. What is so complex or mystical about that?... Oh dear, what have I gone and done! I have talked too much, I have shown too much! I am muddle-headed and tactless! My grandfather once called me that. I thought he was just being affectionate. But in fact I probably *am* tactless. Please... Vladimir!"

Anastasia's voice betrayed a very human concern, and this was probably the reason that almost all my fear of her had now left me. My whole feelings were pre-occupied with the prospect of my son.

"Okay, I'm no longer afraid... Only please try to be a bit more restrained. Remember your grandfather told you that."

"Yes. And grandfather... But here I am talking and talking. I have such a strong desire to tell you everything. Am I a chatterbox? Yes? But I shall try. I shall try very hard to restrain myself. I shall try to speak only in terms you will understand..."

"So, you'll soon be giving birth, Anastasia?" I said.

"Of course! Only, it will not be on time."

"What do you mean, it will not be on time?"

"Ideally it should be in the summertime, when Nature can help with the nurturing."

"Why did you make that decision, if it's so risky for you and the child?"

"Do not worry, Vladimir. At least our son will live."

"And you?"

"And I shall try to hold on till the spring, and everything will adjust itself then."

Anastasia said this without a tinge of sorrow or fear for her life. Then she ran off and jumped into the little lake. The spray of the water in the sunlight took flight, just like fireworks, and landed on the smooth, mirror-like surface of the water. Some thirty seconds later her body slowly began to break the surface. She lay, as it were, on the water, her arms widespread, her palms upturned, and smiled.

I stood on the shore, looked at her and thought to myself: Will the squirrel hear the snap of her fingers when she lies with her baby in one of her shelters? Will she get help from any of her four-footed friends? Will her body have enough heat to warm up the little one?

"If my body should cool off and the baby have nothing to eat, he will start crying," she said quietly, coming out of the water. "His cry of despair may waken Nature, or at least part of it, before the beginning of spring and then everything will be all right. They will nurse him."

"You read my thoughts?"

"No, I just guessed you were thinking about that. That is quite natural."

"Anastasia, you said your relatives live close by. Would they be able to help you?"

"They are very busy, and I must not take them away from their work."

"What are they busy with, Anastasia? What do you do all day long, when in fact you are so completely served by your natural environment?"

"I keep busy... And I try to help people in your world — the ones you call *dachniks* or gardeners."

10

Her beloved dachniks

Anastasia enthusiastically explained to me how many new opportunities could open up for people who communicate with plants. There were two major subjects she talked about not only with particular excitement and animation but, I would have to admit, with a kind of love — namely, bringing up children on the one hand, and *dachniks*[1] on the other. According to everything she said about these people and the importance she attached to them, we would all need to literally bow on our knees before them. Just think! According to her the dachniks have not only managed to save the whole nation from famine, but also sown seeds of good in people's hearts, and are educating the society of the future. There are far too many points to enumerate here — one would need a whole book! And Anastasia kept on arguing, trying to demonstrate this:

"You see, the society you are living in today can learn a lot from communication with the plants to be found around dachas. Yes, I am talking about the dachas, where you personally know every individual plant in your garden-plot, and not those huge, impersonal fields cultivated by monstrous, senseless machines. People feel better when they are working in their dacha plots. Many of them end up living longer. They become kinder. And it is these very dachniks that can pave the way for society to become aware of how destructive the technocratic path can be."

"Anastasia, whether that's true or not is, for the time being, beside the point. What is *your* role in all this? What kind of help can you offer?"

Taking me by the arm, she led me over to the grass. We lay on our backs, the palms of our hands turned upward.

[1]See footnote 4 in Chapter 9: "Who lights a new star?".

"Close your eyes, let go, and try to picture to yourself what I am saying. Right now I'll take a look with my ray and locate, at a distance, some of those people you call dachniks."

After a period of silence, she began to say softly:

"An old woman is unwrapping a piece of cheesecloth in which cucumber seeds have been soaking. The seeds have already begun to develop quite a bit, and I can see little sprouts. Now she has picked up a seed. I have just suggested to her that she should not soak the seeds so much — they will become deformed when they are planted, and this kind of water is not good for them — the seed will go bad. She thinks she herself must have guessed that. And that is partially true — I just helped her guess a bit. Now she will share her idea and tell other people about it. This little deed is done."

Anastasia told how she visualises in her consciousness all sorts of situations involving work, recreation and people's interaction — both with each other and with plants. When the situation she has visualised comes closest to reality, contact is established whereby she can see the person and feel what this person is suffering or sensing. She herself then, as it were, steps into the image of the person and shares her expertise with them. Anastasia said that plants react to people, to Man, with love or hate, and exercise a positive or negative influence on people's health.

"And here is where I have an enormous amount of work to do. I keep myself busy with the dacha garden-plots. The dachniks travel out to their plots, their plantings — they are like their own children — but, unfortunately, their relationship to them is still pretty much on the level of intuition. They still do not have the foundation that comes with a clear realisation of the true purpose behind this relationship.

"Everything — but everything — on Earth, every blade of grass, every insect, has been created for Man, and everything has its individual appointed task to perform in the service of Man. The multitude of medicinal plants are a confirmation of this. But people in your world know very little about how to benefit from the opportunities they are presented with — about how to take full advantage of them."

I asked Anastasia to show some concrete example of the benefits of conscious communication — an example that could be seen, verified in practice and subjected to scientific investigation. Anastasia thought for a little while, then suddenly brightened and exclaimed:

"The dachniks, my beloved dachniks! They will prove it all! They will show what is true and confound all your science! Now how is it I did not think of that or understand it before?"

Some kind of brand new idea made her bubble over with joy.

The whole time I was with her, not once did I see Anastasia sad. She can be serious, thoughtful and concentrated, but more often than not delighting in something. This time her joy literally bubbled over — she jumped up and clapped her hands, and it seemed to me as though the whole forest had become brighter, and begun to stir, responding to her with the rustling of tree-tops and the singing of birds. She whirled round and round, as though she were doing a kind of dance. Then, all radiant, she once again sat down beside me and said:

"Now they will believe! All on account of them, my dear dachniks. They will explain and prove everything!"

Trying to bring her a little more quickly back to the topic of our interrupted conversation, I noted:

"Not necessarily. You say that every insect has been created for Man's benefit, but how can people believe that when they look with so much loathing on the cockroaches crawling over their kitchen tables? What — can it be that they too have been created for our benefit?"

"Cockroaches," declared Anastasia, "will only crawl over a dirty table to collect the remains of any food particles lying about — particles too small for the human eye to see. They process them and render them harmless before discarding them in some secluded spot. If there are too many of them, simply bring a frog into the house and the surplus cockroaches will disappear at once."

What Anastasia went on to propose the dachniks do will probably contradict the principles of the plant sciences — and will certainly contradict the commonly accepted methods of planting and cultivating various garden-plot crops. Her affirmations, however, are so colossal that it seems to me they would be worth trying out for anyone with the opportunity to do so — maybe not throughout their whole plot, but at least in one small section of it, especially since nothing harmful and only good could come of it. Besides, much of what she told me has already been confirmed by the experiments of the biological science expert Mikhail Prokhorov.[2]

[2] *Mikhail Nikolaevich Prokhorov* — Director of ecological programming for a private firm in Moscow, with a doctoral degree in Biology. The author of numerous studies on the interaction of people and plants, Prokhorov speaks about the possibility of the "*direct* influence of human beings on the growth and development of plants and, in certain situations, on the health and behaviour of animals".

11

Advice from Anastasia

The seed as physician

Anastasia stated:

"Every seed you plant contains within itself an enormous amount of information about the Universe. Nothing made by human hands can compare with this information either in size or accuracy. Through the help of these data the seed knows the exact time, down to the millisecond, when it is to come alive, grow — what juices it is to take from the Earth, how to make use of the rays of the celestial bodies — the Sun, Moon and stars, what it is to grow into, what fruit to bring forth. These fruits are designed to sustain Man's life. More powerfully and effectively than any manufactured drugs of the present or future, these fruits are capable of counteracting and withstanding any disease of the human body. But to this end the seed must know about the human condition. So that during the maturation process it can satiate its fruit with the right correlation of substances to heal a specific individual of his disease, if indeed he has it or is prone to it.

"In order for the seed of a cucumber, tomato or any other plant grown in one's plot to have such information, the following steps are necessary:

"Before planting, put into your mouth one or more little seeds, hold them in your mouth, under the tongue, for at least nine minutes.

"Then place the seed between the palms of your hands and hold it there for about thirty seconds. During this time it is important that you be standing barefoot on the spot of earth where you will later be planting it.

"Open your hands, and carefully raise the seed which you are holding to your mouth. Then blow on it lightly, warming it with your breath, and the wee little seed will know everything that is within you.

"Then you need to hold it with your hands open another thirty seconds, presenting the seed to the celestial bodies. And the seed will determine the moment of its awakening. The planets will all help it! And will give the sprouts the light they need to produce fruit especially for you.

"After that you may plant the seed in the ground. In no case should you water it right off, so as not to wash away the saliva which is now covering it, along with other information about you that the seed will take in. It can be watered three days after planting.

"The planting must be done on days appropriate to each vegetable (people already know this, from the lunar calendar). In the absence of watering, a premature planting is not as harmful as an overdue planting.

"It is not a good idea to pull up all the weeds growing in the vicinity of the sprouts. At least one of each kind should be left in place. The weeds can be cut back..."

According to Anastasia, the seed is thus able to take in information about the person who plants it, and then during the cultivation of its fruit it will pick up from the Universe and the Earth the optimum blend of energies needed for a given Man. The weeds should not be disposed of completely, as they have their own appointed function. Some weeds serve to protect the plant from disease while others give supplemental information. During the cultivation time it is vital to communicate with the plant — at least once during its growth period. And it is desirable to approach it and touch it during a full moon.

Anastasia maintains that the fruit cultivated from the seed in this manner, and consumed by the individual who cultivated it, is capable not only of curing him of any diseases of the flesh whatsoever but also of significantly retarding the aging process, rescuing him from harmful habits, tremendously increasing his mental abilities and giving him a sense of inner peace. The fruit will have the most effective influence when consumed no later than three days after harvesting.

The above-mentioned steps should be taken with a variety of plant species in the garden-plot.

It is not necessary to plant a whole row of cucumbers, tomatoes etc., in this manner; just a few plants each is enough.

The fruit of plants grown like this will be distinguished from other plants of the same species not only in taste. If analysed, it will be seen that they are also distinct in terms of the substances they contain.

When planting the seedlings, it is important to soften the dirt in the excavated hole with one's fingers and bare toes, and spit into the hole. Responding to my question "Why the feet?", Anastasia explained that through perspiration from one's feet come substances (toxins, no doubt) containing information about bodily diseases. This information is taken in by the seedlings. They transmit it to the fruit, which will thus be enabled to counteract diseases. Anastasia recommended walking around the plot barefoot from time to time.

"What kind of plants should one cultivate?"

Anastasia replied:

"The same variety that exists in most garden-plots is quite sufficient: raspberries, currants, gooseberries, cucumbers, tomatoes, wild strawberries, any kind of apple tree. Sweet or sour cherries and flowers would be very good too. It does not make any difference how many plants of each kind there are or how big their area of cultivation is.

"There are a few 'definites', without which it would be difficult to imagine a full energy micro-climate: one of them is sunflowers (at least one plant). There should also be one-and-a-half or two square metres of cereal grains (rye or wheat, for example), and be sure to leave an 'island' of at least two square metres for wild-growing herbs — ones that are not planted manually. If you have not left any of them growing around your dacha, you can bring in some turf from the forest and thereby create an island of natural growth."

I asked Anastasia if it were necessary to plant these 'definites' directly in the plot, if there were already some wild-growing herbs close by — say, just beyond the fence — and this is how she responded:

"It is not just the variety of plants that is significant, but also how they are planted — the direct communication with them that allows them to take in the information they need. I have already told you about one of the methods of planting — that's the basic one. The important thing is to infuse the little patch of Nature surrounding you with information about yourself. Only then will the healing effect and the life-giving support of your body be significantly higher than from the fruit alone. Out in the natural 'wilds' (as you call them) —

and Nature really is not wild, it is just unfamiliar to you — there are a great many plants that can help us cure all — and I mean *all* — existing diseases. These plants have been designed for that purpose, but Man has lost, or almost lost, the ability to identify them."

I told Anastasia that we already have many specialised pharmacies which deal in healing herbs, just as there are many physicians and medicine men who make a profession out of herb treatments, and she replied:

"The chief physician is your own body. Right from the start it was endowed with the ability to know which herb should be used and when. How to eat and breathe. It is capable of warding off disease even before its outward manifestation. And nobody else can replace your body, for this is your personal physician, given individually to you by God, and personal only to you. I am telling you how to provide it with the opportunity to act beneficially on your behalf.

"If you make connections with the plants in your garden-plot, they will take care of you and cure you. They will make the right diagnoses all by themselves and prepare the most effective medicine especially designed for you."

Who gets stung by bees?

In every garden-plot there should be at least one colony of bees.

I told Anastasia there are very few people in our society who can communicate with bees. Special training is required, and not everyone is successful.

But she replied:

"A lot of what you do to maintain bee colonies just gets in the way. Over the past centuries there have been only two people on Earth who have come close to understanding this unique life-form."

"And who might they be?"

"They are two monks, who have since been canonised. You can read about them in your books — they can be found in many monastery archives."

"Come on, now, Anastasia! You read church literature too? Where? When? You don't even have a single book!"

"I have at my disposal a much more complete method of retrieving information."

"What kind of method? Again, you're talking in circles! After all, you promised me you wouldn't resort to any mysticism or fantasy."

"I shall tell you about it. I shall even try teaching it to you. You will not understand it right away, but it is simple and natural."

"Well, okay. So, how should bees be kept in a garden-plot?"

"All you have to do is build the same kind of hive for them they would have under natural conditions, and that is it. After that the only thing required is to go to the hive and gather part of the honey, wax and other substances they produce that are so useful for Man."

"Anastasia, that's not simple at all. Who knows what that natural hive should look like? Now, if you could tell me how to do it myself with the materials we have at our disposal, then that might be something feasible."

"All right," she laughed. "Then you will have to wait a bit. I need to *visualise* it, I have to see what people in today's world might have on hand, as you say."

"And where should it be placed so as not to spoil the view?" I added.

"I shall look into that too."

She lay down on the grass as she always did, visualising her — or, rather, our — living situations, but this time I began to observe her carefully. As she lay on the grass, her arms were stretched out in different directions, with palms upturned. Her fingers were partly curled, and their tips (specifically, the tips of the four fingers on each hand) were also positioned so that their soft parts faced upward.

Her fingers first began to stir a little, but then stopped.

Her eyes were closed. Her body was completely relaxed. Her face too appeared relaxed at first, but then a faint shadow of some kind of feeling or sensation moved across it.

Later she explained how seeing at a distance could be practised by anyone with a particular kind of upbringing.

About the beehive, Anastasia had the following to say:

"You need to make the hive in the shape of a hollow block. You can either take a log with a hole in it and hollow it out to enlarge the cavity, or use boards from a deciduous tree to make a long hollow box 120 centimetres long. The boards should be no less than 6 cm thick and the inside measurements of the cavity at least 40 by 40 centimetres. Triangular strips should be inserted into the corners where the inner surfaces meet, to make the cavity somewhat rounded. The strips can be just lightly glued in place, and the bees themselves will firm them up afterward. One end should be fully covered with a board of the same thickness, with a hinged panel at the other end. For this the panel needs to be cut in such a way so that it fits neatly into the opening and sealed with grass or some kind of cloth covering the whole bottom. Make a slit or a series of slits (to provide access for the bees) along the bottom edge of one of the sides approximately one and a half centimetres wide, starting 30 cm from the hinged opening and continuing to the other end. This hive can be set on pilings anywhere in the garden-plot — at least 20–25 centimetres off the ground, with the slits facing south.

"It is even better, however, to set it up under the roof of the house. Then people will not interfere with the bees flying out, and will not be bothered by them. In this case the hive should be aligned horizontally at a 20–30 degree angle, with the opening at the lower end. The hive could even be installed in the attic, provided there is proper ventilation, or on the roof itself. Best of all, though, attach it to the south wall of the house, just under the eaves. The only thing is, you need to make sure you have proper access to the hive so you can remove the honeycomb. Otherwise the hive should stand on a small platform, with an overhead canopy to protect it from the sun, and can be wrapped with insulation in winter."

I remarked to Anastasia that this type of hive could be rather heavy, and the platform and canopy might spoil the appearance of the house. What to do in that case? She looked at me a little surprised, and then explained:

"The thing is that your beekeepers do not really go about it the right way. My grandfather told me about this. Beekeepers today have concocted a lot of different ways of constructing a hive, but all of them involve constant human intervention in its operation — they move the honeycomb frames around within the hive, or move both the hive and the bees to a different spot for the winter, and that is something they should not do.

"Bees build their honeycombs at a specific distance apart to facilitate both ventilation and defence against their enemies, and any human intervention breaks down this system. Instead of spending their time gathering honey and raising offspring, the bees are obliged to fix what has been broken.

"Under natural conditions bees live in tree hollows and cope with any situation perfectly well on their own. I told you that they should be kept under conditions as close to their natural ones as possible. Their presence is extremely beneficial. They pollinate all the plants much more effectively than other agent, thereby increasing the yield. But you must know this pretty well already.

"What you may not know is that bees' mouths open up channels in the plants through which the plants take in supplemental information reflected by the planets — information the plants (and, subsequently, human beings) require."

"But bees sting people, don't you see? How can somebody get a good rest at a dacha if they're constantly afraid of being stung?"

"Bees only sting when people act aggressively toward them, wave them off, become afraid or irritated inside — not necessarily at the bees, but just at anyone. The bees feel this and will not tolerate the rays of any dark feelings. Besides, they may attack those parts of the body where there are channels connecting with some diseased internal organ or where the protective aura has been torn, and so forth.

"You know that bees are already effectively used in treating the disease you call radiculitis, but that is far from being the only thing they can do.

"If I were to tell you about *everything*, especially showing the evidence you are asking for, you would have to spend not just three days but many weeks with me. There is a lot written about bees in your world, all I have done is introduce a few correctives — but please believe me, they are extremely important correctives.

"To establish a colony of bees in a hive like that is very easy. Before introducing a swarm of bees into the hive, put in a little chunk of wax and some honey-plant. You do not need to put in any hand-made frames or cells. Afterward, when there are colonies established on even a few neighbouring dacha plots, the bees will multiply all by themselves; then, as they swarm, they will occupy the empty hives."

"And how should the honey be gathered?"

"Open the panel, break off the hanging honeycomb and extract the sealed honey and pollen. Only do not be greedy. It is important to leave part of it for the bees for the winter. In fact, it is better not to collect any honey at all during the first year."

Hello, Morning!

Anastasia has adapted her morning routine to the conditions of the dacha plot:

"In the morning, preferably at sunrise, walk out to the garden-plot barefoot, and approach any plants you like. You can touch them. This does not have to be done in accord with some sort of schedule or ritual to be strictly followed day after day, but simply as one feels moved, or as one desires. But it should be done before washing. Then the plants will sense the fragrances of the substances emitted by the body through the pores of the skin during sleep.

"If it is warm and there is a small grassy patch close by (and it would be helpful if there were), lie down there and stretch out for three or four minutes. And if some little bug should happen to crawl onto your body during this time, do not chase it away. Many bugs open up pores on the human body and cleanse them. As a rule, they open up the pores through which toxins are expelled and all sorts of internal ailments are brought to the surface, allowing the person to wash them away.

"If there is any pond water on the plot, you should immerse yourself in it. If not, then you can pour water over yourself as you stand barefoot close to the plants and seedbeds or, even better, between the beds — or, for example, one morning alongside the raspberry bushes, the next by the currant bushes etc. And after washing you should not dry off right away. You should shake off the water drops from your hands, spreading them onto the surrounding plants. And use your hands to brush off the water from other parts of your body. After this you can go through the usual procedures of washing and using any conveniences to which you are accustomed."

Evening routine

"In the evening, before going to bed it is important to wash your feet, using water with the addition of a small quantity (a few drops) of juice from saltbush or nettles — or the two together — but no soap or shampoo. After washing your feet, pour the water onto the seedbeds. Then, if necessary, you can still wash your feet with soap.

"This evening routine is important for two reasons. As the feet perspire, toxins come to the surface, removing internal diseases from the body, and these must be washed away to cleanse the pores. Juices from saltbush or nettles are good at facilitating this process. In pouring the remaining water onto the seedbeds, you are giving supplemental information to the plants and microorganisms about your current state of well-being.

This is very important too. Only after receiving this information can our visible and invisible environment work out and pick up from the Universe and the Earth everything it needs for the normal functioning of your body."

It will prepare everything by itself

I was still interested in knowing what Anastasia had to say about food. After all, she has a rather unique dietary régime, and so I asked:

"Anastasia, tell me how you think a person should feed himself — what should he eat, how often during the day and in what amounts? Our world pays a great deal of attention to this question. There's a huge quantity of all sorts of literature on this subject, health-food recipes, advice on losing weight..."

"It is difficult to picture human beings' lifestyle any other way under the circumstances currently imposed by the technocratic world. The dark forces are constantly trying to take the natural operating system of this world — the one given to humanity right from the start — and substitute their own cumbersome artificial system which goes against human nature."

I asked Anastasia to put it in more concrete terms, without her philosophical musings, and she continued:

"You know, these questions of yours as to what, when and how much a person should eat — they are best answered by the individual's own body. The sensations of hunger and thirst are designed to send a signal to each particular individual indicating when he should take in food. This precise moment is the right one for each person. The world of technocracy, being incapable of affording each individual the opportunity of satisfying his hunger and thirst at the moment desired by his body, has tried to force him into its own schedule based on nothing but this world's own helplessness, and then attempts to justify this compulsion in the name of some sort of 'efficiency'.

"Just think: one person spends half the day sitting down, expending hardly any energy, while another exerts himself with some kind of physical labour, or simply runs and perspires all over, thereby using up many times more energy, and yet both are expected to eat at exactly the same time. A person should take in food at the moment advised by his body, and there can be no other advisor. I realise that under your world's conditions this is practically impossible, but the opportunity does exist for people at their dachas with their attached garden-plots, and they should take advantage of it and forget about their unnatural, artificial régimes.

"The same applies to your second question: *What* should one eat? The answer is: whatever is available at the moment — whatever is on hand, so to speak. The body itself will select what it needs. I could offer you a bit of non-traditional advice: if you have a household pet like a cat or a dog, keep track of its movements carefully. Occasionally it will find something in the way of grasses or herbs and eat it. You should tear off a few samples of whatever it selects and add it to your diet. This is not something you have to do every day — once or twice a week is sufficient.

"You should also take it upon yourself to gather some cereal grain, thresh it, grind it into flour and then use the flour to bake bread. This is extremely important. Anyone consuming this bread even once or twice a year will build up a store of energy capable of awakening his inner spiritual powers — not only calming his soul but also exerting a beneficial influence on his physical condition. This bread can be shared with relatives and close friends. If shared with sincerity and love, it will have quite a beneficial influence on them as well. It is very helpful to every individual's health to spend three days, at least once each summer, eating only what is grown in his garden-plot, along with bread, sunflower oil and just a pinch of salt."

I have already described Anastasia's own eating habits. While she was telling me all this, she would unwittingly tear off a blade of grass or two, put it in her mouth and chew it, and offer me some too. I decided to give it a try. I can't say the taste was anything to write home about, but neither did it provoke any sense of distaste.

It seems as though Anastasia has left the whole task of nourishment and life-support up to Nature; she never allows it to interrupt her train of thought, which is always busy with some more important issue. Even so, her health is as remarkable as her outward beauty, of which it is an inseparable part. According to Anastasia, anyone who has established such a relationship with the Earth and the plants on his own plot of land, has the opportunity of ridding his body of absolutely every kind of disease.

Disease *per se* is the result of Man distancing himself from the natural systems designed to take care of his health and life-support. For such systems, the task of counteracting any disease presents no problem whatsoever, since this is their whole reason for being. However, the benefits experienced by people who have set up such information-exchange contacts with a little patch of the natural world go far beyond dealing with diseases.

12

Sleeping under one's star

I have already mentioned how animated Anastasia becomes when talking about plants and people who communicate with them. I thought that, living in Nature as she did, she might have studied Nature alone, but she also possesses information about planetary relationships. She literally feels the celestial bodies. See for yourself what she has to say about sleeping under the stars:

"Once plants have received information about a specific person, they embark upon an information exchange with cosmic forces, but here they are simply intermediaries, carrying out a narrowly focused task involving one's fleshly body and certain emotional planes. They never touch the complex processes which, out of all the animal and plant world on the planet, are inherent only in the human brain and on human planes of existence. Nevertheless, this information exchange they establish allows Man to do what he alone can do — namely, interact with the Intelligence of the Universe or, more precisely, to exchange information with this Intelligence. An altogether simple procedure permits him not only to do this, but also to feel the beneficial effect of such interaction."

Anastasia described this procedure as follows:

"Pick an evening when weather conditions are favourable and arrange to spend the night under the stars. You should situate your sleeping place close to raspberry or currant bushes, or to beds where cereal seeds have been planted. You should be there alone. As you lie with your face to the stars, do not close your eyes right away. Let your gaze, physically and mentally, wander across the celestial bodies. Do not become tense while thinking about them. Your thought must be free and unencumbered.

"First, try to think about those celestial bodies which are visible to your eye; then you can dream about what you treasure in life, about the people closest to you, people for whom you wish only good. Do not attempt to even think at this point about seeking revenge or wishing evil upon anyone, for that might have a negative effect on you. This uncomplicated procedure will awaken some of the many little cells dormant in your brain, the vast majority of which never wake even once during a person's whole lifetime. The cosmic forces will be with you and help you attain the realisation of your brightest and most unimaginable dreams, will help you find peace in your heart, establish positive relationships with your loved ones, and increase — or call into being — their love for you.

"It is useful to try repeating this procedure a number of times. It is effective only when carried out at the location of your constant contact with the plant world. And you will feel it yourself as early as the next morning. It is especially important to go through this procedure on the eve of your birthday. To explain how all this works would take too long right now, and is not important. Parts of the explanation you would not believe, other parts you would not understand. It can be discussed much more quickly and easily with people who are already trying it and feeling its influence on themselves, since the information, once received and verified, will facilitate the reception of any information that follows."

13

A helper and mentor
for your child

In asking Anastasia how a plot of ground with seed-plantings, even plantings carried out in the special manner she described and maintaining close contact with Man, could facilitate the raising of children, I expected to hear an answer something like: 'Children need to be imbued with a love of nature.' However, I was wrong. What she actually said was amazing both in its simplicity of argument and in the depth of its philosophical implications.

"Nature and the mind of the Universe have seen to it that every new Man is born a sovereign, a king! He is like an angel — pure and undefiled. Through the still soft upper part of his head he takes in a huge flood of information from the Universe. The abilities inherent in each newborn child are such as to allow him to become the wisest creature in the Universe, God-like. It takes him very little time to bestow grace and happiness upon his parents. During this period — amounting to no more than nine earth-years — he becomes aware of what constitutes creation and the meaning of human existence. And everything that he needs to accomplish this already exists. Only the parents should not distort the genuine, natural structure of creation by cutting the child off from the most perfect works in the Universe.

"The world of technocracy, however, does not allow parents to do the right thing. What does an infant see with his first conscious glance around? He sees the ceiling, the edge of his crib, some patches of fabric, the walls — all attributes and values of the artificial world created by a technocratic society. And in this world he finds his mother and her breasts.

"'This must be the way things are!' he concludes. His smiling parents offer him toys and other objects that rattle and squeak, as though they were priceless treasures. Why? He will spend a long time trying to make sense of this rattling and squeaking. He will try to comprehend them both through his conscious mind and his sub-conscious. And then these same smiling parents will try wrapping him up in some kind of fabric, which he finds most uncomfortable. He will make attempts to free himself, but in vain! And the only means of protest he has at his disposal is a cry! A cry of protest, an appeal for help, a cry of rebellion. And from that moment on this angel and sovereign becomes an indigent slave, begging for handouts.

"One after another the child is presented with the accoutrements of an artificial world. He is rewarded for his acceptance by some new toy or item of clothing. And along with this the thought is drummed into him that these are the dominant objects in the world where he has arrived. Still in his infancy, despite his status as the most perfect being in the Universe, he is pandered to and treated as an imperfect creature, even in those institutions you consider educational, where again he is constantly reminded of the values of this artificial world. Not until the age of nine does he hear a passing mention of the existence of the world of nature, and then only as an adjunct to that other, more important world of manufactured objects. And most people are never afforded the opportunity to become aware of the truth, even to the end of their days. And so it seems as though the simple question 'What is the meaning of life?' goes unanswered.

"*The meaning of life* — that is to be found in truth, joy and love. A nine-year-old child brought up in the natural world has a far more accurate perception of creation than all the scientific institutions of your world or, indeed, many of your prominent scholars."

"Stop, Anastasia! You probably have in mind a knowledge of nature, assuming his life proceeds along the same lines as yours. Here I can agree with you. But think: today's Man is obliged (rightly or wrongly — that is another question) — but he is obliged to live specifically in our technocratic world, as you call it. Someone brought up as you propose will certainly know nature, and have a feeling for it, but in everything else he will be an utter ignoramus. Besides, there are other sciences, like mathematics, physics, chemistry — or simply just knowing about life and its societal manifestations."

"For someone who has learnt at the right time about what constitutes creation, those things are mere trifles. If he wants, or considers it necessary to prove himself in some scientific field, he will easily surpass all others."

"How could that happen so quickly?"

"Man in the world of technocracy has never yet invented anything that is not already present in nature. Even the most perfect manufactured devices are but a poor imitation of what exists in nature."

"Well, that may be. But you promised to explain how a child could be raised and his capabilities developed in *our* conditions. Only talk about this in a way I can understand, using concrete examples."

"I shall try to be more concrete," replied Anastasia. "I have already visualised situations like this and have tried to hint to one family what they should do, only there was no way they could have grasped the crucial point and asked their child the proper questions... These parents turned out to have an unusually pure, talented child, who could have brought tremendous benefit to people living on Earth.

"So, these parents arrive with this three-year-old child at their dacha plot and bring along his favourite toys. Artificial toys which displace the true priorities of the Universe. Oh, if only they had not done that! Just think, the child could have been occupied and entertained with something far more interesting than senseless and even harmful interaction with manufactured objects.

"First of all, you should ask him to help you, only ask him in all seriousness, without any pandering, especially since he will actually be able to offer you assistance. If you do any planting, for example, ask him to hold the seeds in preparation for sowing, or rake out the seedbeds, or have him put a seed into the hole you have prepared. And in the process talk to him about what you are doing, something like this:

"'We will be putting the little seed into the ground and covering it with earth. When the sun in the sky shines and warms the earth, the little seed will get warm and start to grow. It will want to see the sun, and a little shoot will poke its head out of the earth, just like this one.' At this point you can show him some little blade of grass. 'If the seed likes the sunshine, it will grow bigger and bigger and maybe turn into a tree, or something smaller, like a flower. And I want it to bring you tasty fruit, and you will eat it if you like it. The little shoot will prepare its fruit for you.'

"Whenever you arrive with your child at the dacha plot, or when he awakes first thing in the morning, have him look and see whether any new shoots have come up. If you should notice one, show your delight. Even when you are putting young plants rather than seeds into the ground, it is important to explain to your child what you are doing. If you are planting tomato seedlings, for example, let him hand you the stalks one by one. If a stalk should inadvertently break, take the broken stalk into your hands and say: 'I do not think this one will live or bear fruit, since it is broken, but let us try planting it anyway.' And plant at least one of the broken ones right along with the others.

"A few days later, when you visit the seedbed again with your child and the stalks have firmed up, point out the broken, withering stalk to your little one and remind him that it was broken during the planting, but do not use any preaching tone of voice in doing so. You need to talk with him as an equal. You should bear in mind the thought tnat he is superior to you in some respects — in the purity of his thought, for example. He is an angel! If you succeed in understanding that, you can then proceed intuitively, and your child will indeed become a person who will happify your days.

"Whenever you sleep under the stars, take your child with you, lay him down beside you, let him look at the stars, but under no circumstances tell him the names of the planets or how you perceive their origin and function, since this is something you do not really know yourself, and the theories stored in your brain will only lead the child astray from the truth. His sub-conscious knows the truth, and it will penetrate his consciousness all by itself. All you need to do is to tell him that you like looking at the shining stars, and ask your child which star he likes best of all.

"In general, it is very important to know how to ask your child questions. The next year you can offer your child his own seedbed, fix it up and give him the freedom to do whatever he likes with it. Do not ever compel him by force to do anything with it, and do not correct what he has done. You can simply ask him what he likes. You can offer help, but only after asking his permission to work along with him. When you are planting cereal grains, have him throw some grains on the seedbed for you."

"Okay," I remarked to Anastasia, still not fully convinced. "Maybe a child like this will show interest in the plant world and maybe he'll become a good agronomist, but where is he going to get knowledge from in other areas?"

"What do you mean, *where from?* It is not just a matter of having a knowledge and feeling about what grows and how. The main thing is that the child is starting to think, analyse, and cells are awakening in his brain which will operate throughout his life. They will make him brighter and more talented compared to those whose corresponding cells are still dormant.

"As far as 'civilised' life goes — what you call *progress* — he may well turn out to be superior in any field of endeavour — all the more so since the purity of his thought will make him an exceptionally happy person. The contact he has established with his planets will allow him to constantly take in — and *exchange* — more and more information. The incoming messages will be received by his sub-conscious and transmitted to his consciousness in the form of many new thoughts and discoveries. Outwardly he will look like everyone else, but inwardly... This is the kind of Man you call a genius."

14

Forest school

"Tell me, Anastasia, is this the way *your* parents brought *you* up?"

She responded after a brief pause, during which, I gathered, she was recollecting her childhood.

"I remember practically nothing of my Papa or Mama in the flesh. I was brought up by my grandfather and great-grandfather pretty much as I have explained to you. But, you see, I myself had a good feeling very early on for Nature and the animal world around me — perhaps I was not aware of all the details of how it operated, but that is not the important thing when one has a feeling for it. Grandfather and Great-Grandfather would approach me from time to time and ask questions and expect me to answer them. In our culture, older generations treat an infant or young child virtually as a deity, and use the child's responses as a check on their own purity."

I began asking Anastasia to recall some specific question and answer. She smiled, and told me:

"Once I was playing with a little snake. I turned around, and there were Grandfather and Great-Grandfather standing right beside me, smiling. I was very delighted, since it was always interesting being with them. They are the only ones who can ask me questions and their hearts beat in the same rhythm as mine, but with animals it is different. I ran over to them. Great-Grandfather bowed to me, while Grandfather took me on his knees. I listened to his heart beat and I fingered the hairs on his beard as I examined them. Nobody spoke. We were thinking together, and it was good that way. Then Grandfather asked me:

"'Tell me, Anastasia, why do you think my hair grows here and here,' pointing to the top of his head and his beard, 'and not here?' pointing to his nose and forehead.

"I touched his nose and forehead, but no reply was forthcoming. I could not give an unthinking answer — I had to understand it.

"The next time they came, Grandfather again said:

"'Well, I am still thinking, why my hair grows here, and not here,' again indicating his nose and forehead.

"Great-Grandfather looked at me seriously and attentively. Then I thought: perhaps it is really a serious question with him, and I asked:

"'Grandfather, what is it? Do you really want your hair to grow everywhere, even on your nose and forehead?'

"Great-Grandfather began pondering the question, while Grandfather replied:

"'No, not really.'

"'Then that is why your hair does not grow there, because you do not want it to!'

"He reflected on that, stroking his beard, and mused, as though he were putting the question to himself: 'And if it grows here, that means it is because I want it to?'

"I confirmed his thought:

"'Of course, Grandfather, not only you, but I, and the one who thought you up.'

"At this point Great-Grandfather asked me rather excitedly:

"'And who was it that thought him up?'

"'The one who thought everything up,' I replied.

"'But where is he, show me!' Great-Grandfather asked, bowing to me.

"I could not give him an answer right away, but the question stayed with me, and I started thinking about it often."

"And did you eventually give him an answer?" I asked Anastasia.

"I gave him an answer about a year later, and then he started asking me more questions, but up until the time I gave the answer, neither Grandfather nor Great-Grandfather had asked me any new questions, and I began to get very concerned."

15

Attentiveness to Man

I asked Anastasia who taught her to speak and converse, if she had almost no memory of her father and mother and her grandfather and great-grandfather talked with her only rarely. The answers she gave were quite a shock to me, and require interpretation by specialists, and so I shall try to reproduce them as fully as I can. Their meaning has gradually begun to sink in for me. She responded to my first question with a question of her own:

"Do you mean the ability to speak in different people's languages?"

"How do you mean, 'different'? What, you can speak more than one language?"

"Yes," she replied.

"Including German, French, English, Japanese, Chinese?"

"Yes," she repeated, and then added: "You can see I speak your language."

"You mean Russian?"

"Well, that is too general. I speak, or at least try to speak, using words and phrases you yourself use when you talk. At first it was a little challenging for me, since your vocabulary is not very large and you repeat yourself a fair amount. Nor do you have much expression of feeling. That is not the kind of language which easily lends itself to accurately saying everything one wishes to say."

"Wait, Anastasia — I'm going to ask you something in a foreign language, and you give me an answer."

I said *Hello* to her in English, and then in French. She answered me right off.

Unfortunately I myself have not mastered any foreign language. In school I studied German, but with rather poor marks. I did remember one whole sentence in German, which my schoolmates and I learnt by rote. I recited it to Anastasia:

"Ich liebe dich, und gib mir deine Hand."[1]

She extended her hand to me and answered in German:

"I give you my hand."

Amazed by what I had heard, and still not believing my ears, I asked:

"So then, any person can be taught any language?"

I had an intuitive feeling that there must be some kind of simple explanation for this extraordinary phenomenon, and I had to know what it was so I could tell others about it.

"Anastasia, perhaps you could explain this in my language, and try to do it with examples, so that I can understand," I asked somewhat excitedly.

"All right, all right, only calm down and let go, or you will not understand. But let me first teach you to write in Russian."

"I know how to write. You tell me about teaching foreign languages."

"I do not mean just handwriting — I shall teach you to be a writer. A very talented writer. You shall write a book."

"That's impossible."

"It *is* possible! It is quite simple."

Anastasia took a stick and outlined on the ground the whole Russian alphabet along with the punctuation marks, and asked me how many letters there were.

"Thirty-three," I replied.[2]

"You see, that is a very small number of letters. Can you call what I have outlined a book?"

"No," I answered. "It's just an ordinary alphabet, that's all. Ordinary letters."

"Yet all the books in the Russian language are made up of these ordinary letters," Anastasia observed. "Do you not agree? Do you not see how simple it all is?"

---

[1]"I love you, and give me your hand."

[2]*Thirty-three* — This is the correct number of letters in the modern Russian version of the Cyrillic alphabet. It is believed that Cyrillic was adapted from Greek by the monk St. Cyril in the ninth century to introduce the Gospels to the Slavic-speaking peoples of the Balkan peninsula. It later spread to all Slavic lands (including Russia) where the Orthodox Church predominated. The number of letters in the alphabet varies from language to language. In other areas, under the influence of the Roman Catholic Church, the Latin writing system was adapted to the local Slavic language.

"Yes, but in books they're — they're arranged differently."

"Correct, all books consist of a multitude of combinations of these letters. People arrange them on the pages automatically, guided by their feelings. And from this it follows that books originate not from a combination of letters and sounds, but from feelings outlined by people's imagination. The result is that the readers are aroused by approximately the same feelings as the writers, and such feelings can be recalled for a long time. Can you recollect any images or situations from books you have read?"

"Yes, I can," I replied, after a moment's thought.

For some reason I recalled Lermontov's[3] *Hero of our time,* and began to tell the story to Anastasia. She interrupted me:

"You see, you can still depict the characters from this book and tell me what they felt, even though quite a bit of time has gone by since you read it. But if I were to ask you to tell me in what sequence the thirty-three letters of the Russian alphabet were set forth in that book, what combinations they were arranged in, could you do that?"

"No. That would be impossible."

"Indeed, it would be very difficult. So, feelings have been conveyed from one Man to another with the help of all sorts of combinations of these thirty-three letters. You looked at these combinations of letters and forgot them right off, but the feelings and images remained to be remembered for a long time.

"So it turns out that if emotional feelings are directly associated with these marks on paper without thinking about any conventions, one's soul will cause these marks to appear in just the right sequence and combinations so that any reader may subsequently feel the soul of the writer. And if in the soul of the writer..."

"Wait, Anastasia. Speak more simply, more clearly, more specifically, show me through some kind of an example how languages are

---

[3] *Mikhail Yurevich Lermontov* (1814–1841) — after Alexander Pushkin, Russia's second most-loved classic poet, who also had several novels and stories to his credit, including *Hero of our time (Geroi nashego vremeni).* A descendant of a Scottish military officer, Captain George Learmont, who had entered the Russian service in 1613, Lermontov (an officer himself) came to prominence especially after writing an inflammatory poetic eulogy on Pushkin when the latter was killed in a duel ("Death of a poet", 1837). Ironically, Lermontov himself was killed in a duel only four years later.

to be taught. You can make me into a writer later on. Tell me first: who taught *you* to understand different languages and how."

"My great-grandfather," replied Anastasia.

"Give me an example," I asked, anxious to understand everything in a hurry.

"All right, but do not be concerned. I shall still find a way to help you understand, and if it is that important to you, I shall try teaching all the languages to you too. It is simple, after all."

"For us it's quite incredible, Anastasia. So do try to explain. And tell me, how much time will it take to teach me?"

She thought for a moment, looked at me, and then said:

"Your memory is not very good, and then there are your domestic problems... You will need a lot of time."

"How long?" I was impatient for an answer.

"For everyday comprehension of phrases such as *Hello* and *Good-bye,* I would say it will take at least four months, possibly six," she replied.

"Enough, Anastasia! Tell me how your great-grandfather did it."

"He played with me."

"How did he play? Tell me."

"Calm down! Let go! I cannot understand why you are so impatient!"

And then she quietly went on:

"Great-Grandfather played with me, as though he were joking with me. Whenever he came to me all by himself, without Grandfather, he would always approach me, bow at the waist, and hold out his hand to me, and I would hold out mine to him. He would first shake my hand, then get down on one knee, kiss my hand and say 'Hello, Anastasia!'

"One time he came, he did everything as usual, his eyes looked at me tenderly as usual, but his lips were saying some kind of abracadabra. I looked at him in surprise, and he said something else, equally unintelligible. I could not take it any longer and asked:

"'Granpakins, have you forgotten what to say?'

"'Yes, I have,' Great-Grandfather answered. Then he stepped away from me a few paces, stopped to think about something and came over to me again, extended his hand to me and I held out mine to him. He dropped on one knee and kissed my hand. His look was gentle, his lips were moving, but no sound was coming out.   I was even a bit afraid.   Then I decided a reminder might help.

"'Hello, Anastasia!' I hinted.

"'Correct!' Great-Grandfather confirmed with a smile.

"At that point I realised it was a game — he and I would often play games together after that.   At first it was quite simple, but then the game became more complicated, and more fascinating.   It is a game that begins when one is three years old and goes on until the age of eleven, when one undergoes a kind of test.   This involves looking attentively at the person you are talking with and being able to understand what they are saying, no matter what language they are expressing it in.   This kind of dialogue is far superior to speech — it is more rapid and conveys far more information.   You would call it thought-transfer.   You think it is abnormal, something out of fantasy, but it is simply an attentive attitude toward Man, drawing upon a developed imagination and a good memory.   It involves not just a more efficient method of information exchange, but getting to know a person's soul, along with the animal and plant world, and what constitutes creation as a whole."

"Anastasia," I said, "what do plants growing in a garden-plot have to do with this — what is their role in all this?"

"What do you mean, what have they to do with it?   At the same time as the child is getting to know the world of plants as a part of the functioning of the Universe, he is also entering into contact with his planets.   With their help and the help of his parents he quickly, very quickly, gets to know the truth and develops intensively in the fields of psychology, philosophy and the natural sciences — your disciplines.   But if the game goes on and some kind of man-made object from the artificial world is used as an example, the child will become lost.   He will not receive any assistance from the powers of Nature or the Universe."

"I have already noted, Anastasia, that in the final analysis such a child could become an agronomist.   Now where would his knowledge come from in other areas?"

But Anastasia maintained that a Man raised in such a manner would show an aptitude for quick learning in any of our scholarly disciplines.

16

Flying saucers?
Nothing extraordinary!

Then I asked her to show me an example of her knowledge of some technical subject.

"You want me to tell you how all the different machines of your world operate?"

"The kind of thing our prominent scientists are only touching the fringes of. Why don't you make some great scientific discovery, let's say?"

"That is what I have been doing for you the whole time you have been here."

"Not just for me, for the world of science — a discovery they would be prepared to recognise. Go ahead, make a verifiable discovery in some technical field — like space ships, the atom, automobile fuel — since you say it's all so simple."

"In comparison with what I have just shown you, those fields you mention are something like, to use a term from your language, the stone age!"

"That's perfect! Something you consider primitive, but at least I'll be able to understand it. You can prove you're right and show evidence that your intelligence is superior to mine. Tell me, for example, what you think of our aeroplanes and space ships — pretty close to perfect machines?"

"No. They are altogether primitive, they only serve to show how primitive the technocratic path of development is."

That remark put me on my guard, since I realised that either her conclusions were those of a madwoman, *or* she really knew far more than someone with an ordinary consciousness could ever imagine. I continued my questioning:

"What do you mean when you say our rockets and planes are primitive?"

Anastasia responded after a brief pause, as though allowing time for her words to sink in.

"The functioning of all your machines, every single one of them, is based on the energy of explosion. Not knowing any more efficient natural sources of energy, you resort to such primitive, awkward substitutes with incredible stubbornness. And even the destructive consequences of their use do not stop you. The range of your aeroplanes and rockets is simply laughable — according to the scale of the Universe they rise a wee tiny bit above the Earth, and now this method has practically reached its ceiling, do not you agree? But that is ridiculous! An exploding or burning substance propels some monstrous structure that you call a space ship. And the greater part of this ship is designed precisely to 'solve' this problem of propulsion."

"And what might be an alternative principle of movement through the atmosphere?"

"A flying saucer might be a good example," Anastasia responded.

"What?! You know about flying saucers and their propulsion systems?"

"Of course I know. It is very simple and rational."

I felt my throat go dry, and tried to hurry her up.

"Tell me, Anastasia, quickly... and in a way I can understand."

"All right, only do not get excited — it will be harder to understand when you are excited. The propulsion principle of a flying saucer is based on the energy of generating a vacuum."

"How so? Be more precise!"

"You have a limited vocabulary, yet I am compelled to restrict myself to it so that you can understand me."

"Well, I'll add to it!" I blurted out in agitation. "I'll add words like *jar, lid, tablet, air*..." and I began to quickly name all the words that just popped into my head at that moment, and even let out a few swearwords.

Anastasia broke in:

"You need not bother — I already know all the words you can express yourself with, but there are still others, and besides that, there is whole different method of conveying information. If I used that, I could explain everything to you in a minute. As things stand now, it may take an hour or two. That is a lot, and I really wanted to tell you about something else, something much more meaningful."

"No, Anastasia. Tell me about flying saucers and their propulsion methods, tell me about energy carriers. Until I understand that, I shan't listen to anything else."

"All right," she acquiesced, and then went on. "An explosion occurs when a solid substance quickly changes under a definable influence into gaseous form, or when, in the course of a reaction, two gaseous substances evolve into something even lighter. Everyone, of course, understands this part."

"Yes," I replied. "If powder is ignited it becomes smoke, and liquid fuel becomes gas."

"Yes, more or less. But if you or your people had purer thoughts and consequently a knowledge of the functionings of Nature, you would have long ago become aware that if there is a substance capable of instant expansion and, through explosion, transformation into another state, the opposite process must also hold true.[1] In Nature there are living microorganisms that transform gaseous substances into solids. All plants do this in fact, only at varying speeds and with varying degrees of firmness and solidity of the resulting substance.

"Take a look around you, and you will see that plants take in liquid from the earth and breathe air, and then process these into a hard and solid body — let us say, wood, or something even harder and more solid, like a nut-shell or a plum-stone. A microorganism smaller than the eye can see does this with fantastic speed, feeding, it would seem, on air alone. It is these same kinds of microorganisms that power flying saucers. They are like the microcells in the brain, only their operation has a very narrow focus. Their sole function is propulsion. But they carry out this function to perfection and they can accelerate a flying saucer to one-nineteenth the speed of the average modern Earth-dweller's thought.

"These microorganisms are located on the inner surface of the upper part of the flying saucer and positioned between its double

[1]Many non-traditional scientists have criticised the generating of energy from explosion or the burning of fuel as unnatural and destructive. One of them, the so-called 'water wizard' Viktor Schauberger (1885–1958), an illustrious Austrian forester and engineer, has spoken — in terms very similar to those used by Anastasia here — of the 'energy of *implosion*' — as a natural alternative to today's destructive technologies. Schauberger has gained deep insights into the workings of Nature and, among other things, was involved in research on the use of implosion (or energy from a vacuum) for propulsion. For a fascinating account of Schauberger's work in eco-technology, forestry, water purification and other areas, see Callum Coats' book *Living energies*.

walls, which are set approximately three centimetres apart. The upper and lower surfaces of the outer walls are porous, with micro-sized pinholes. The microorganisms draw in air through these pinholes, thereby creating a vacuum ahead of the saucer. The streams of air begin to congeal even before contact with the saucer, and as they pass through the microorganisms they are transformed into tiny spheres. Then these spheres are enlarged even more, to approximately half a centimetre in diameter. They lose their firmness, and slide down between the walls into the lower part of the saucer, where they again decompose into a gaseous substance. You can even eat them, if you can do this before they decompose."

"What about the walls of the flying saucer — what are they made of?"

"They are cultivated — grown."

"How so?"

"Why the surprise? Just give it a little thought, you will figure it out. Many people cultivate a fungus in various kinds of containers.[2] The fungus imbues the water in which it is placed with a pleasant, slightly acidic flavour, and takes the shape of the container. This fungus is very similar to a flying saucer; it creates a double wall around itself. If another microorganism is added to its water, it produces a congealment, but this so-called microorganism can be produced — or, rather, generated — by the power of the will, or the brain, much like a vivid concept or imagery."

"Can you do this?" I asked.

"Yes, but I don't have sufficient power of my own. The action of several dozen people having the same ability is required, and it takes about a year all told."

"And can one find on our Earth everything necessary to make — or grow, as you say — such a flying saucer and the microorganisms?"

---

[2]This fungus, famous for its medicinal properties, is known as *Kombucha* (*Medusomyces gisevii*). It looks like a pile of pancakes or a flat multi-layered jellyfish (its scientific name is actually derived from the German word for 'jellyfish' — *meduse*), floating on top of the water in the container in which it is placed and eventually assuming the form of that container. The fungus is cultivated in sweetened weak tea. The result is a pleasant-tasting drink used both as a refreshment and as a cure for a great number of diseases. In Russia this fungus is commonly cultivated by people in large glass jars on their kitchen window sills.

"Of course one can. The Earth has everything that the Universe has."

"But how do you get the microorganisms inside the walls of the saucer if they are so small you can't even see them?"

"Once the upper wall is cultivated, it will attract and collect them in huge numbers, just as bees are attracted to cells. But this process also requires the collective will of several dozen people. In any case, what is the use of elaborating further if you cannot cultivate it for lack of people with the right kind of will, intelligence and knowledge?"

"Isn't there some way *you* could help?"

"I could."

"So, do it!"

"I have already."

"What have you done?" I was still perplexed.

"I told you how children should be raised. And I can tell you more. You must tell this to others. Many will understand, and their children raised in this manner will have the intelligence, knowledge and will permitting them to make not only a primitive flying saucer, but significantly more..."

"Anastasia, how do you know so much about flying saucers? Does that too come through your communication with plants?"

"They have landed here, and I, well, I helped the occupants repair their ship."

"Are they much smarter than us?"

"Not at all. They have a long way to go to attain the level of Man — they are afraid of us, afraid to approach people, even though they are very curious. At first they were afraid of me. They trained their mental paralysers on me. Put on quite a show. They tried to frighten me, shock me. It was quite a challenge to calm them down and convince them I would only treat them with affection."

"Well, how can they be less smart than us if they can do things Man can't do yet?"

"What is so surprising about that? Bees too make incredible structures out of natural materials, including whole ventilation and heating systems, but that does not mean they are superior to Man in intelligence. In the Universe there is no one and nothing stronger than Man except God!"

17

The brain —
a supercomputer

The possibility of building a flying saucer greatly interested me. If one examines the principle of propulsion just as a hypothesis, it is still a new one. A flying saucer, however, is a complex machine and is not a high-priority item for us earthlings.

For that reason I wanted to hear something that would be understandable right away. I wanted a 'something' that did not require any investigation of scholarly minds, but could be immediately put into practice in our daily lives and benefit everyone. I began asking Anastasia to come up with a solution to a question that our society was being confronted with today. She agreed, but asked:

"Could you at least put it in more specific terms, this question? How can I solve something when I do not know what you have in mind?"

I began thinking: What was the number one problem we faced today, and the following terms came to mind:

"You know, Anastasia, our major cities right now are confronted with a most acute problem — environmental pollution. The air in these cities is so bad it's hard to breathe."

"But you yourselves are the ones polluting it."

"We realise that. Please, hear me out, only don't go philosophising about how we must be purer ourselves, have more trees around and so forth. Just take things as they are today and think up something — for example, how to reduce the pollution in our major cities by fifty percent without costing the treasury — the government, that is — any extra money. And make it so that your plan will be the most logical of all possible alternatives, and that it will be capable of instant implementation so that I and everyone else cannot fail to understand it."

"I shall try at once," Anastasia replied. "Have you specified all the terms?"

I thought I should try and make it even more complex, just in case her mind and abilities really turned out to be truly superior to what our own powers of reasoning allowed. So I added:

"And make whatever you think up to be profit-generating!"

"For whom?"

"For me, and for the country too. You live within the borders of Russia, so make it the whole of Russia."

"Are we talking about money?"

"Yes."

"An enormous amount of money?"

"Profit, Anastasia — well, money — is never an enormous amount. But I need enough money to be able to pay for this expedition and have enough left over for a new one. And as for Russia..."

I thought for a moment... I thought: What if Anastasia were even a little interested in the material benefits of our civilisation, and then asked:

"You wouldn't want anything for yourself?"

"I have everything," she replied.

But all at once an idea came to me — something that might possibly interest her.

"How about this, Anastasia: let's have your plan make enough money to provide free seeds — or at least seeds at a discount — to all your beloved dachniks, or gardeners, throughout Russia!"

"Terrific!" Anastasia exclaimed. "What a wonderful idea! If you have finished, I shall now get to work. How delightful that sounds! Seeds... Or... is there anything else you wish to add?"

"No, Anastasia, that's enough for now."

I felt her inspiration and excitement not only over the task itself, but especially over the free seeds for her dachniks. Yet I still felt convinced that even with her special abilities a solution to the problem of air pollution was simply out of the question, else our many scientific institutions would have come up with one long ago.

With a bustle of energy this time, not her usual calm and quiet self, Anastasia lay down on the grass, her arms widespread. Her curled fingers reached their cushioned tips upward, alternating between motion and stillness, while her eyelids trembled on her closed eyes.

She lay there for about twenty minutes, then opened her eyes, sat up and said:

"I have determined the nature of the problem. But what a nightmare it is!"

"What have you determined, and what's this about a nightmare?"

"The greatest harm is coming from your so-called automobiles. There are so many of them in the large cities and every one of them is emitting both an unpleasant odour and substances harmful to human bodies. The most frightening thing is that these substances are mixing with earth- or dust-particles, and impregnating the dust. The movement of the automobiles picks up the impregnated dust, and people are breathing in this horrible mess. It gets swept into the air, and then settles on the grass and the trees, covering everything around. This is very bad. It is very harmful to the health of both people and plants."

"Of course it's bad. Everybody knows it's bad, only nobody can *do* anything about it. We have street-cleaning machines, but they can't keep up. You, Anastasia, have discovered absolutely nothing new, you haven't thought up any original solution to purify our air."

"All I did just now was to determine the basic source of the danger. Now I shall think about it further and analyse it... I need to concentrate for a long time, perhaps as long as an hour, since I have never dealt with a problem like this before. So that you will not be bored, do go for a walk in the forest or..."

"You get on with your thinking. I'll find something to do."

And Anastasia withdrew into herself. Coming back an hour later, after a walk in the forest, I found her, as it appeared to me, in a state of some discontent, and I said:

"You see, Anastasia, you and that brain of yours aren't capable of doing anything either. Only don't worry about it — we've got a lot of scientific institutions working on this question. But they, just like you, can only describe the fact that pollution is going on. They haven't been able to do anything about it yet."

She answered in a somewhat apologetic tone:

"I have gone over in my mind, I believe, all the possible variants, but I do not see any way of quickly reducing the pollution by fifty percent."

My mind was at once set on the alert: she had found some sort of solution after all.

"So, what kind of reduction did you come up with?" I asked.

She sighed.

"Not that much. I managed to achieve... thirty-five to forty percent."

"What?!" I couldn't help exclaim.

"Pretty poor result, eh?" asked Anastasia.

A lump formed in my throat, I realised she was incapable of lying, exaggerating or downplaying anything she said. Trying to restrain my excitement, I said:

"Let's change the terms of the project — let's say thirty-eight percent. Quick, tell me what you've come up with."

"Your automobiles must be equipped to not only scatter this foul dust, but to collect it as well."

"How can we do that? Talk faster!"

"Those things sticking out in front of the automobiles, what are they called?"

"Bumpers?" I offered.

"All right, bumpers. Inside them or below them should be attached a little box with small holes facing frontwards. There should also be holes on its back side, so that air can escape. While the automobiles are in motion, air laden with this harmful dust will be drawn in through the front holes, purified, and then escape through the back holes, and that air will already be twenty percent less polluted."

"And what about the remaining twenty percent?"

"Right now virtually none of this dust is removed, but with this method there will be a lot less of it in the air, since it will be collected all over the place every day. I have calculated that in one month, with the help of these little boxes, if they are fitted on all automobiles, the amount of polluting dust will decrease by forty percent. Beyond that there will be no reduction, since other factors are at work."

"What size of boxes, and what should they contain? How many holes and at what distance from each other?"

"Vladimir, perhaps you would like me to personally attach them to every single automobile?"

For the first time I perceived that Anastasia had a sense of humour, and I began to laugh at the thought of her attaching her little boxes to all the cars. She laughed too, delighting in my cheerful mood and began whirling her way across the glade.

The principle was really very simple — the rest was merely a matter of technology. Already, without Anastasia's help, I was beginning to imagine how it could all be: orders from administrative heads, motor-vehicle inspection control, turning in old filters for new ones at filling stations, a system of vouchers and so forth. A routine regulation, just like seat-belts.

All it had taken back then was one stroke of the pen, and presto! — seat-belts in every family car. And here too, one stroke of the pen, and, again, presto! — cleaner air! And there would be tough competition among entrepreneurs for orders to supply the boxes, a good deal of work for the manufacturing plants, and the main thing, of course, cleaner air!

"Wait," I said, turning once more to Anastasia, who was still whirling around in a boisterous dance.

"What should be put into those boxes?"

"Into those boxes... into those boxes... You will come up with a little something. It is very simple," she replied, without stopping.

"And where is my money going to come from, and to supply seeds for the dachniks?" came another question.

She stopped.

"What do you mean, where from? You wanted my idea to be the most rational of all — and that is exactly what I have thought up: the most rational solution there can be. It will spread to large cities throughout the world and for this idea they will pay Russia enough to supply the free seeds, and enough to pay you. Only you will receive your payment under certain conditions."

I didn't pay attention immediately to her remark about the 'certain conditions', but began focusing in on something else:

"So, we should patent it? Otherwise who would pay of their own free will?"

"Why would they not pay? They will pay, and I can even set the rates right now. From the production of these boxes, Russia will get two percent, and you will get one hundredth of a percent."

"What's the good of your setting the rates? You do have a few strong points, but when it comes to business you're still a complete ignoramus. Nobody will pay voluntarily. Even when there are signed agreements they don't always pay. If only you knew how many there are in our world that don't![1] Our arbitration courts are overloaded. By the way, do you know what an arbitration court is?"

"I can guess. But in this case they will pay faithfully. Anyone who does not pay will go bankrupt. Only honest people will prosper."

"What will make them go bankrupt? Don't tell me you're in the racket business?!"

"What *are* you imagining now? Think about it! They themselves — or rather, circumstances themselves will overtake any cheaters and *make* them go bankrupt."

And then the thought dawned on me — given that Anastasia is incapable of lying and, as she herself said, the systems inherent in Nature do not allow her to make a mistake: it means that before stating any conclusions, she must have processed in her brain an enormous amount of information, made zillions of mathematical calculations, and taken into account a whole mass of psychological characteristics of the people who would be participating in her project. In our terms, she not only solved the most difficult question of purifying the air, but also drew up and analysed a business plan, and all that in roughly an hour and a half. I thought I had still better clarify certain details, and so I asked her:

"Tell me, Anastasia, you made some sort of calculations in your head, figuring out the percentage of pollution reduction, and the amount of money to be realised from the sale of your car-accessory boxes, filter replacements and so forth?"

"Calculations were made — in the greatest detail — and not just with the help of the brain..."

---

[1]Following Russia's liberal economic reforms of 1992 (including abandonment of governmental control over prices and cessation of subsidies to unprofitable industries) the country witnessed a run-away inflation and disruption of existing economic ties, resulting in mass unemployment, widespread bankruptcies, delays in salary payments of six months or more, and a crisis of non-payments between enterprises (goods shipped and services rendered from one business to another but not paid for), which paralysed the national economy.

"Stop! Quiet! Let me tell you what I think... Does this mean you could compete with our top-of-the-line computers — let's say, Japanese or American computers?"

"But that's not very interesting," she replied, adding: "That is primitive and somewhat degrading. Competing with a computer — that is tantamount to... oh, how can I find you a good analogy? That is tantamount to hands or feet competing with a prosthesis — and not even with a full prosthesis, but just part of one. With the computer the most vital element is missing. And that most vital element is... *feelings*."

I started to argue the opposite, telling how in our world there are people considered very intelligent, respected in society, that play chess with computers. But when this and other arguments still failed to convince her, I started asking her to agree to do this for me and other people as a proof of the possibilities of the human brain. She finally agreed, and then I made the invitation more specific:

"So, I can officially announce your willingness to take part in a problem-solving contest with a Japanese supercomputer?"

"Why a Japanese?" Anastasia countered.

"Because they are considered to be the best in the world."

"Well now! It will be better if I do it with all of them at once, so you will not have to ask me again to do such a boring thing!"

"Great!" I exclaimed enthusiastically. "Let's do it with all of them, only you'll have to think up a problem."

"All right," Anastasia reluctantly agreed. "But for a start, so as not to waste time on thinking one up, let them try solving the problem you put to me earlier, and see whether they confirm or refute my hypothesis. If they refute it, let them put forth their own. Let us be judged by life and by other people."

"Great, Anastasia! Good for you! That is most constructive. And how much time, do you think, should be allowed for them to come up with a solution? I think the hour and a half you took will not be enough for them. Let's give them three months."

"Three months it shall be."

"And I suggest the judging be left to anybody who wants to take part. If there're a lot of judges, then no one can influence the outcome for their own ulterior motives."

"So be it, but I would still like to talk with you about raising children..."

Anastasia considered the raising of children paramount and would always delight in talking about it. She wasn't particularly excited about my idea of competing with computers. However, I was very happy to have secured her co-operation. Now I want to invite all firms producing state-of-the-art computers to join a competition to solve the above-stated problem.

I still felt I had to clarify a point or two with Anastasia.

"And what prize should be offered to the winner?" I asked.

"I do not need anything!" she replied.

"Why did you think just of yourself? Are you so absolutely certain you're going to win?"

"Of course. I am Man, after all."

"Well, okay. What can you offer the firm who takes first place after you?"

"Well, I could give them some advice on how to perfect their primitive computer."

"Then it's settled."

18

"In him was life; and the life was the light of men"

The Gospel of John

Upon my request Anastasia took me to see the ringing cedar which her grandfather and great-grandfather had talked about. It was not very far from the glade. The tree, approximately forty metres tall, rose slightly higher than its neighbours, but its principal distinguishing feature was the aureole radiating from its glistening crown — similar to the halos around the faces of saints depicted on icons. The aureole was not even — it pulsated, and at its upper tip one could see a thin ray of light beaming into the infinity of the heavens.

The spectacle was dazzling and absolutely charming.

At Anastasia's suggestion I pressed the palms of my hands to its trunk. I could hear a ringing or crackling noise, comparable to what one might hear standing under a high-voltage transmission line, only more resonant.

"It was I who happened to discover a way to send its energy back into Space and then have it distributed here on Earth," Anastasia told me. "You see how its bark has been torn off in various places. That is where the bear was climbing it. It was quite a challenge to get her to carry me up to the first branches. I clung on to the fur on her neck. She would climb and then let out a roar, climb and roar. After reaching the lowest branches, I was able to clamber up from branch to branch, right to the top. I sat there for two days and thought of everything I could to save the tree. I stroked the tree, and shouted up into the sky, but nothing helped.

"Then Grandfather and Great-Grandfather arrived. You can imagine the scene — there they were standing down below, reprimanding me and demanding that I climb down. I in turn demanded that they tell me what could be done with the tree. How to save the ringing cedar, since nobody was cutting it down. They did not speak. But I felt that they knew the answer. Grandfather, old trickster that he was, tried to lure me down, promising to help me establish a connection with a certain woman I had been unable to reach on my own.

"This was a woman I very much wanted to help. Earlier Grandfather would only be annoyed by my desire to spend so much time on her instead of doing other things. But I knew that he could not help me, as Great-Grandfather had twice tried to do this behind Grandfather's back, and he failed too.

"At that point Grandfather really began putting up a fuss. He seized hold of a branch, ran around the cedar tree and beat the air with the branch, shouting that I was the most hare-brained member of the family, that I was acting illogically, that I refused to accept sound advice and that he would give my bottom a good whipping. And again he beat the air with the branch. Now that was a real humdinger of a threat, and even Great-Grandfather burst out laughing. I too gave a hearty laugh. In doing so I inadvertently broke a branch at the top, and a glow began emanating from it. And I heard Great-Grandfather's voice, serious, commanding and entreating all at the same time:

"'Don't touch anything more, little one. Come down very carefully. You've already done enough!'

"I obeyed and climbed down. Great-Grandfather silently embraced me. Trembling all over, he pointed at the tree, on which more and more branches were beginning to glow. Then a ray formed, pointing upward. Now the ringing cedar would not burn up — through its little ray it would give everything it had saved up for the past five hundred years to people and to the Earth. Great-Grandfather explained that the ray had formed in the exact spot where I had shouted upward and had inadvertently broken a branch while I was laughing. Great-Grandfather said that if I had touched the ray emanating from the broken branch, my brain would have exploded, as there was too much energy and information in this little ray. That was exactly how my Papa and Mama had perished..."

Anastasia put her hands on the mighty trunk of the ringing cedar she had saved, and pressed her cheek against it. After pausing for a while, she continued her story.

"They, my Papa and Mama, once came upon a ringing cedar just like this one. Only Mama had been doing everything a little differently, since she did not know. She had climbed up into a neighbouring tree, from which she reached out and touched one of the lower branches of the ringing cedar and broke it off, inadvertently exposing herself to the ray which flamed up out of the broken branch. The branch had been pointing downward, and the ray went down into the Earth. It is very bad, very harmful, when such energy falls into the Earth.

"When Papa came, he saw this ray, and saw my Mama, who had been left hanging, one hand still firmly grasping the *ordinary cedar* branch. In the other hand she held the broken branch of the *ringing cedar.*

"Papa, no doubt, had an immediate grasp of everything that had happened. He climbed up the ringing cedar, right to the top. Grandfather and Great-Grandfather saw him break off the upper branches, but they did not glow, while more and more of the lower ones began glowing. Great-Grandfather said that Papa realised that it would not be long before he would never be able to climb down. The upward-beaming ray with its pulsating glow failed to appear. All that was going on was more and more thin rays shining downward. An upward ray did appear when Papa broke off a large branch pointing up. And even though it was not glowing, he bent it and pointed it at himself.

"When it did flame up, Papa still managed to unclasp his hands, the branch straightened and the ray from the branch directed itself toward the sky, and then the pulsating aureole formed.

"Great-Grandfather said that at the last moment of his life Papa's brain was able to take in an enormous flood of energy and information, and that he was able, in some incredible way, to clear his mind of all previously accumulated information, and so was able to gain the time required to unclasp his hands and direct the branch upward just before his brain exploded."

Anastasia once more stroked the cedar trunk with her hands, once more pressed her cheek against it and stood stock still, smiling, listening to the ringing of the cedar.

"Anastasia, that cedar nut oil, are its healing properties stronger or weaker than the pieces of the ringing cedar?"

"The same. Provided the nuts are gathered at the proper time and with the proper attitude toward the cedar. Provided the tree bestows them of itself."

"Do you know how to do that?"

"Yes, I do."

"Will you tell me?"

"All right. I shall tell you."

19
The need to change one's outlook on the world

I asked Anastasia about the woman over whom she had a disagreement with her grandfather. I asked her why she had been unable to establish a connection with her and why she thought this contact was necessary.

"You see," Anastasia began her story, "it is very important, when two people join their lives together, that they have a spiritual attraction to each other. Unfortunately, everything basically starts with the carnal. For example, you see a beautiful girl and desire to be close to her. You still have not seen the individual — the Man — or her soul. Very often people join their destinies together only on the basis of carnal attraction. Either that quickly passes or it is transferred to someone else. What then keeps people together?

"To find a kindred spirit with whom one can attain true happiness is not all that complicated. Your technocratic world, however, puts up massive interference. The woman I am trying to reach lives in a large city, and regularly travels to the same place each day — probably to her work. Either there or on the way she finds or meets up with a man who is very close to her spirit, one with whom she could be really happy and, most importantly, one with whom she could bear a child capable of bringing so much good into the world. Because they would create this child with the same impulsion as we did.

But there is no way this man can bring himself to tell this woman that he loves her, and she herself is partly to blame for this. Just think: he looks into her face and sees, as it were, his heart's desire, the apple of his eye, while she, as soon as she feels someone's gaze upon her, perks up right away, and "unwittingly" tries to lift her skirt higher. And so on. This man is at once carnally aroused, but he does not know her well, and so he then goes to someone he is better acquainted with, someone he feels is more accessible, but still led on by these same carnal desires.

s

"I want to suggest to this woman what she should do, but I cannot break through to her. Her brain will not open to the awareness of new information, even for a second. It is constantly pre-occupied with issues of day-to-day living. Can you imagine, one time I followed her for a whole twenty-four hours! What a terrible sight! Grandfather then got upset with me for not working enough with the dachniks and for spreading myself too thin, and sticking my nose in where it does not belong.

"When this woman wakes in the morning, her first thought is not to delight in the coming day but how to prepare something to eat. She gets upset over some missing food item, and then gets upset over something you smear on your face in the morning, like face-cream or rouge. She spends her whole time thinking how she is going to get it. She is always late and is constantly on the run, trying not to miss first one form of transport and then the next.

"At her regular destination her brain is overloaded with — how shall I put it — all sorts of *nonsense,* at least from my point of view. On the other hand it is supposed to give her face a business-like expression and fulfil the job tasks she is assigned. All this while she is thinking about one of her girlfriends or acquaintances and getting angry at them. At the same time she is listening to everything going on around her. And, can you imagine, the same routine is repeated day after day like clockwork.

"On her way home, when people notice her, she can put on the appearance of an almost happy woman. But she is continually thinking about problems, or her make-up, or looking at clothes in shop windows — above all, clothes that will expose her alluring charms, supposing that this will result in some kind of miracle, except in her case everything happens the wrong way around. She gets home and starts house-cleaning. She thinks she is relaxing when she watches her television and prepares her meals, but the main thing is, she thinks about good things only for a split second. Even when she goes to bed, she is still mulling over her daily cares and stays in the same mental rut.

"If only she could turn away from her thoughts even just for a moment during the day and think of..."

"Wait, Anastasia! Explain specifically how you see her, her outward appearance and clothing, and tell me what she should be thinking about at the moment when this man is with her. What should she do to make him at least attempt to tell her he loves her?"

Anastasia explained everything in the minutest detail. I shall only mention here what I consider to be the most important points.

"Her dress should come to just below the knee. It should be green with a white collar and no cleavage. She should wear hardly any make-up, and listen with interest to the person talking to her."

"And that's it?" I remarked upon hearing such a simple explanation.

To which Anastasia remarked:

"There is so much underlying these simple instructions. In order for her to choose that particular dress, change her make-up and look at that person with genuine interest, she will have to change her whole outlook on the world."

20

A mortal sin

"I still need to tell you, Vladimir, about the terms under which you will receive money in the bank, when there will be a great deal of money in your accounts."

"Go ahead, Anastasia, it will be a pleasant experience," I replied.

However, I was devastated by what I heard. Judge for yourselves: here is what she set forth:

"In order to withdraw the money from your bank account, you must meet the following conditions: first of all, for three days before receiving it you must not drink anything alcoholic. When you arrive at the bank, the manager must verify, with the help of the devices you have, your compliance with this condition in the presence of not less than two witnesses. If this first condition is met, you may then proceed to carry out the second: you must do no less than nine deep knee-bends in front of the bank manager and the two witnesses present."

When the significance — or rather, the absurdity — of her words finally sunk in, I jumped up, and she stood up as well. I couldn't believe my ears and countered:

"First they're going to check my alcohol content, and then I am to do at least nine deep knee-bends like this, is that it?"

"Yes," responded Anastasia. "And for each knee-bend they will be able to release from your account no more than one million of your roubles at their present worth."

I was overwhelmed by a sense of rage, anger and annoyance.

"What did you say that for? Well, what for?! I was feeling so good. I believed you. I was starting to think that you were right about a lot of things, that there was logic in your arguments. But you... Now I am absolutely convinced that you're a schizophrenic, a stupid hick, a mad woman! This latest thing you said has wiped out everything else. It's completely devoid of any sense or logic — that's not just my opinion, any sane person would agree with me. Ha! Don't tell me you still want me to write out these conditions in your book?"

"Yes."

"Now you've really gone mad. Do you mean to tell me you were planning to write out instructions to the banks or publish this order?"

"No. They will read it in the book, and they will act accordingly with you. Otherwise they can expect to go bankrupt."

"Oh, my God!!! And I've been listening to this creature three days already? Don't tell me you would like the bank manager to do knee-bends with me too in the presence of witnesses?"

"It would be good for him, as it will be for you. But for them I have not set such strict conditions as I have for you."

"So, you're only doing this for *my* benefit? Do you have the slightest idea what a mockery you've made of me? See what the love of a crazy recluse can spill over into! Only it won't work — not one single bank will ever agree to serve me under those conditions, no matter how much you have visualised such a situation. In your dreams, eh?! Well, you can stand here and do all the deep knee-bends you want, you nincompoop!"

"The banks will agree and whether you know it or not will open accounts for you — granted, only those banks which are willing to operate ethically, and people will trust them and come to them," Anastasia went on, not budging an inch from her position.

I found myself becoming increasingly irritated and angry. Angry with myself or angry at Anastasia. Come on now, think how long I've listened to her, trying to understand what she was saying, and here she's turned out to be simply half-crazy. I started laying into her, using, to put it mildly, some pretty coarse language.

She stood there, leaning with her back to a tree, her head just slightly bowed. One hand was clasped to her chest, the other was raised upward, lightly waving.

I recognised that gesture. She used it every time she needed to bring calm to the surrounding natural environment so I wouldn't get fearful of it, and I realised why she needed to calm them down on this occasion.

Every insulting or coarse word directed at Anastasia felt like a whip cracking against her flesh, making her whole body tremble.

I fell silent. I sat down again on the grass, turned away from Anastasia, deciding I'd better calm down myself and head back to the riverbank, and not talk with her any more at all. But when I heard her voice call out behind me, I was amazed that it didn't have the slightest hint of resentment or rebuke:

"You know, Vladimir, everything bad that happens to Man is brought on by Man himself, whenever he disobeys the laws of spiritual being and breaks his connection with Nature.

"The forces of darkness try to distract their attention with the instant attraction of your technocratic way of life, to make them forget the simple truths and commandments set forth way back in the Bible. And they all too often succeed.

"One of the mortal sins of Man is pride. Most people are subject to it, this sin. I shall not at the moment go into all the terrible, disastrous effects it produces. After you return home and try to make sense of it, you will understand, either on your own or through the help of enlightened individuals who come to see you. For now I shall just say this: the forces of darkness, which are diametrically opposed to the forces of light, are every moment working to make sure Man does not let go of this sin, and money is one of their basic tools in this campaign.

"They were the ones that thought up this concept of money. Money is like a high-tension zone. The forces of darkness are proud of this invention. They even think themselves stronger than the forces of light for having come up with money. And for being able to use money to distract people from their true purpose.

"This great confrontation has lasted for millennia, and Man is at its centre. But I do not want *you* to be enslaved to this sin.

"I realise that mere explanations are not enough to settle this question. Because in spite of thousands of years of explanations mankind has not understood nor discovered the means of counteracting this sin. It is only natural that you would not be able to discover it either. But I really, very much, want to save you from this mortal danger which can corrupt the spirit. That is why I thought up a special situation just for you, one that would cause this device of the forces of darkness to be broken, or fail, or even work the opposite way, for the extermination of the sin.

"That is why they have become so enraged. Their anger has been implanted in you, and you for your part started shouting your insults at me. They wanted to make me angry at you in return, but I will never do that. I realised that what I thought up would hit the mark precisely, and now it is clear that their system which has worked flawlessly for thousands of years can indeed be broken. Right now I have done this only for you, but I shall think up something for other people too.

"Now what harm is there in drinking less of that alcoholic poison and in becoming less arrogant and stubborn? What were you so upset over? Of course, it was pride that was upsetting you."

She fell silent, and I thought: Improbable as it is, her brain — or something besides — may have put into this comic, utterly abnormal situation of doing deep knee-bends in a bank such a deep meaningfulness that there really could be some logic in it. I'd better think about this a little more calmly.

All my anger at Anastasia passed and, in its place, arose a feeling of uneasy guilt. However, instead of apologising on the spot, I simply turned to her with a desire for reconciliation. Anastasia, it turned out, felt my inner state. She at once gave a joyful shudder all over and began talking at top speed.

21

Touching Paradise

"Your brain is tired of listening to me, and yet I still have so much I want to tell you. I do so want to... But you need to rest. Let us sit again for a little while."

We sat down on the grass. Anastasia took me by the shoulders and drew me close to her. The back of my head touched her breasts, which gave me a pleasant warm feeling.

"Do not be afraid of me, let yourself go," she quietly said and lay down on the grass so that it would be more comfortable for me to rest. She ran the fingers of one of her hands through my hair, as if combing them, while the fingertips of her other hand quickly touched my forehead and temples. Occasionally she would lightly press down with her fingernails at various points on the top of my head. All this gave me a feeling of tranquillity and enlightenment. Then, putting her hands on my shoulders, Anastasia said:

"Listen now... and please tell me what sounds you hear around you."

I listened, and my hearing caught a wide range of sounds, all different in tonality, rhythm and continuity.

I began naming the sounds aloud: the birds singing in the trees, the chirping and clicking of insects in the grass, the rustle of the leaves, the fluttering and flapping of birds' wings. I named everything I could hear, then fell silent and went on listening. This was pleasant and very interesting for me.

"You have not named everything," Anastasia observed.

"Everything," I replied. "Well, maybe I left out something not very significant or something I didn't catch — not anything important, that is."

"Vladimir, do you not hear how my heart is beating?" asked Anastasia.

Could I really have not been paying attention to this sound? The sound of her heart beating?

"Yes," I hastened to respond. "Of course I hear it, I hear it very well, it is beating evenly and calmly."

"Try to memorise the intervals of the various sounds you hear. You can choose the principal sounds and memorise them."

I selected the chirping of some insect, the cawing of a crow and the gurgling and splash of the water in the stream.

"Now I shall increase the tempo of my heartbeat and you listen to see what happens all around."

Anastasia's heartbeat increased in frequency, and right away the rhythm of sounds I could hear around me joined in with a heightened tonality.

"That's astounding! Simply incredible!" I exclaimed. "What are you saying, Anastasia, are they so sensitive to the rhythm of your heartbeat?"

"Yes. Everything — absolutely everything: a little blade of grass, a big tree, even the bugs — they all react to any change in the rhythm of my heart. The trees accelerate their inner processes, and work harder to produce oxygen."

"Is this how all the plants and animals in people's environment react?" I asked.

"No. In your world they do not understand to whom they should react, and you do not try to make contact with them. Besides, you do not understand the purpose of such contact, and do not give them sufficient information about yourself.

"Something similar might happen between plants and the people who work on their little garden-plots, if only people would do everything I outlined to you, imbue the seed with information about themselves and begin to communicate more consciously with their plants. Do you want me to show you what Man will feel when he makes such contact?"

"Of course I want you to. But how will you do that?"

"I shall tune the rhythm of my heartbeat to yours, and you will feel it."

She slid her hand inside my shirt. Her warm palm lightly pressed against my chest. Little by little her heart adjusted its tuning and began beating in the same rhythm as mine. And something most amazing happened: I felt an unusually pleasant sensation, as though my mother and my relatives were right there beside me. A sense of softness and good health came over my body, and my heart was filled with joy, freedom and a whole new sense of creation.

The range of surrounding sounds caressed me and communicated the truth — not a truth comprehensible in all its detail, just something I felt intuitively. I had the impression that all the pleasing and joyous feelings I had ever experienced in my life were now merging into a single and wonderful sensation. Perhaps it is this sensation that is called *happiness*.

But as soon as Anastasia began to change the rhythm of her heart-beat, the wonderful sensation started to leave me. I asked:

"More! Please, let me feel it some more, Anastasia!"

"I cannot do that for long, after all, I have my own rhythm."

"Even just a little bit more," I pleaded.

And once again Anastasia brought back the sensation of happiness, just for a short time, and then everything faded, but not without leaving me with a small taste of the pleasant and radiant sensation as a memory of it. We remained silent for a while, and then I felt like hearing Anastasia's voice again, and I asked:

"Was it this good for the first people — Adam and Eve? You just lie around, enjoy life and prosper — everything at hand?... Only it can become boring if there's nothing to do."

Instead of answering my question, Anastasia asked one of her own:

"Tell me, Vladimir, do many people think of Adam, the first Man, as you thought just now?"

"Probably the majority. But what was there for them to do, in Paradise? It was only later that Man started to develop and thought up everything. Man developed through labour. He became smarter thanks to labour."

"Yes, labour is needful, but the first Man was infinitely smarter than his descendants today, and his labour was more meaningful, it demanded considerable intelligence, awareness and will."

"But what did Adam do in Paradise? Did he tend a garden? That is something that can be done today by any gardener, not to mention plant-breeding specialists! Nothing more is said in the Bible about Adam's activity."

"If the Bible told everything in detail, it would be impossible to read through it in a single human lifetime. One must *understand* the Bible — there is so much information behind each verse. Do you want to know what Adam did? I shall tell you. But first, remember that it is the Bible that tells us that God assigned Adam to give names and specify the purpose of every creature living on the Earth. And he — Adam — did this. He did what all the scientific institutions in the world taken together have not yet been able to do."

"Anastasia, do you turn to God yourself, do you ask Him for anything for yourself?"

"What more can I ask, when so much has already been given me? It is my task to thank Him and help Him."

22

Who will bring up our son?

On the way back to the river, as Anastasia was escorting me to my motorboat, we sat down to rest in the place where she had left her outer clothing, and I asked her:

"Anastasia, how will we bring up our son?"

"Try to understand, Vladimir: you are not yet ready to bring him up. And when his eyes first take in a conscious awareness of the world, you should not be there."

I seized her by the shoulders and gave her a shaking.

"What are you saying? What liberties are you taking here? I can't understand how you could have come to such one-sided conclusions. Anyway, even though the mere fact of your existence is incredible, that doesn't give you the right to decide everything yourself and in violation of all the rules of logic!"

"Calm down, Vladimir, please. I do not know what logic you have in mind, but do try and make sense of it, calmly."

"What am I to make sense of? The child is not only yours, he's mine too, and I want him to have a father, I want him to be well taken care of, and get an education."

"Please understand, he does not need any kind of material benefits, as you see them. He will have everything he needs right from the start. Even in his infancy he will be taking in and making sense of so much information that your kind of education will be simply ludicrous. It's the same as sending a learned mathematician back to Grade One.

"You want to bring the baby some kind of senseless toy, but he has absolutely no need of it whatsoever. You are the one who needs it for your own self-satisfaction: 'Oh look at me, I'm so good and caring!' If you think that you will do some good by offering your son a car or anything else along that line, well, he can get it himself just by wishing for it. Be calm and think about something specific you could tell your son, think about what you could teach him, think about what you have done in life that he might find interesting."

Anastasia continued talking in soft, quiet tones, but her words still made me tremble.

"You see, Vladimir, when he begins to make sense of creation, you will look like an underdeveloped creature next to him. Do you really want that, do you really want your son to see you standing there like a dimwit? The only thing that can bring the two of you together is your level of mental purity, but few attain that level in your world. You must strive to attain it."

I realised that it was absolutely useless to argue with her, and I cried out in despair.

"Does that mean he'll never know anything about me?"

"I shall tell him about you, about your world, when he is able to comprehend it in a meaningful way and make his own decisions. What he will do then, I do not know."

Despair, pain, resentment, fearful conjecture — all these swirled around in my brain. I felt like smashing this beautiful intellectual recluse's face with all my might.

I understood everything. And what I understood left me breathless.

"It's all clear! Now it's all clear to me! You... You had nobody to bang with to give you a child. That business at the beginning — that was all just an act, you sly vixen! You made yourself into a nun! You needed a child. But you *did* go to Moscow. She "sold her mushrooms and berries". Ha! You could have got yourself a shag there right on the street. All you had to do was take off that jacket and shawl of yours and you would have had takers right off. Then you wouldn't have needed to spin your web and trap me in it.

"Of course! You needed a man who was dreaming about a son. And you've got yours! Did you ever think about the child? About your son? One destined in advance to live the life of a recluse. To live the way *you* think he should. Come on now, here she's been sounding off about 'the truth'. You've got an awful lot of gall, you hermit!

"What is it with you — truth as a last resort? Well, did you ever think about me? Me! *I* dreamt about a son! I dreamt about passing along my business to him. I'd teach him to be a businessman. I want-ed a son to love. And now how am I supposed to live? To live and know that your precious little son is crawling around unprotected somewhere out in the wilds of the taiga? With no future. With no father. That's what breaks my heart. But that's not something you can understand, you forest bitch!"

"Perhaps," Anastasia quietly responded, "your heart will gain the awareness it needs and everything will be all right? A pain like that will cleanse the soul, accelerate thought and summon you to creation."

But I was still burning with rage and anger. I wasn't in control of myself. I grabbed a stick. I ran away from Anastasia and began beating the stick against a small tree with all my might until the stick broke.

Then I turned to look at Anastasia standing there and... oh, how she appeared to me! Incredibly, the anger started to leave. I thought to myself: oh, now I've gone and done it again — I lost control of myself and went wild. Just like the last time, when I swore at her.

Anastasia was standing there against a tree, one arm stretched upward, her head bent forward, as though withstanding the onslaught of a hurricane. With my anger completely gone, I went closer and began looking at her. Now her hands were clasped to her chest, her body slightly trembling. She didn't speak, only her kind, kind eyes were looking at me with the same tenderness as before. We stood there that way for some time, just looking at each other. And I started reflecting along these lines:

There's no doubt about it — she is incapable of lying.

She didn't have to say anything, but...

She knew it would be hard, and yet she spoke. Of course, that too is a challenge. How can you possibly live if you must always tell the truth, and say only what you think?! But what can you do if that's the way she is and can't be anything else?

What's done is done. Everything happened the way it happened. Now she will be the mother of my son.

She *will* be a mother, if she said so. Of course, she'll be a pretty strange mother. That lifestyle of hers... And her way of thinking... Oh, well, there's nothing to be done with her.

Still, she's physically very strong. And kind. She really knows Nature well, knows the animals. And she's smart. In her own peculiar way, at least.

In any case she knows a lot about raising children. She kept wanting to talk about children the whole time. She'll nurture the boy. Somebody like her will definitely nurture him. She'll get him through the cold, through snowstorms even. They mean nothing to her. She'll nurture him, yes indeed. And she'll bring him up right.

And somehow I've got to adapt to the situation. I'll come and see them in the summertime, like going to a dacha. No way in the winter — I wouldn't make it. But in the summer I can play with my son. He'll grow up, and I'll tell him about people in big cities...

At any rate, this time I've got to apologise to her...

And I said:

"I'm sorry, Anastasia, I got nervous again."

And right off she said:

"You are not to blame. Only do not be hard on yourself. Do not worry. After all, you were concerned about your son. You were afraid that things would turn out bad for him, that the mother of your son was just an ordinary bitch. That she could not love with real human love. But you must not worry. You must not get upset. You talked that way because you did not know, you did not know anything about my love, my darling."

23

Through a window of time

"Anastasia, if you are so smart and omnipotent, that means you could help me?"

She looked up at the sky, and then again at me.

"In the whole of the Universe there is no being capable of more powerful development and greater freedom than Man. All other civilisations bow before Man. All sorts of civilisations have the capability of developing and bringing themselves to perfection, but only in one direction, and they are not free. Even the greatness of Man is beyond their grasp. God — the Great Mind — created Man and to no one else gave He more than to Man."

I could not make sense — at least right off — of what she was saying. And again I uttered the same question, pleading for help, not fully understanding what kind of help I needed.

She asked me:

"What is it that you have in mind? Do you want me to cure all your physical ailments?

"That is a simple matter for me. I already did this six months ago, only in the principal area of need no benefit came about: the dark and destructive elements common to people of your world have not lessened in you. And your various aches and pains are trying to come back again... 'You witch, mad-woman hermit, get out of here this instant!' you're probably thinking, right?"

"Yes," I answered in amazement. "That is exactly what I was thinking — you read my mind?"

"I surmised that that is what you might be thinking. Indeed, it is written all over your face. Tell me, Vladimir, do you not... well... remember me, at least a little?"

The question dumbfounded me, and I began carefully examining her facial features. Especially her eyes. I really began to think that I might have seen them somewhere before, but where?

"Anastasia, you said yourself that you spend all your time in the forest. How then could I have seen you?"

She gave me a smile and ran off.

A short while later Anastasia came out from behind the bushes dressed in a long skirt, a brown buttoned cardigan, her hair done up in a shawl. But without the quilted jacket in which she had greeted me on the riverbank. And the shawl was tied differently. Her clothes were clean, though not stylish, and her shawl covered her forehead and neck... and I remembered her.

24

A strange girl

The summer before, our convoy ship had docked at one of the villages not far from these parts. We needed to buy bulk meat for the restaurant and spend some time in port.

Sixty kilometres farther on there would be a particularly dangerous section of the river, which meant our ship could not travel through there at night (certain sections of the river were not equipped with navigation lights). So as not to waste time, we began announcing over our outdoor loudspeaker system as well as the local radio that we were throwing a party that evening aboard our vessel.

The sleek white ship standing at the dock, glistening with a huge array of lights, and alive with the music pouring forth from it inevitably attracted the young people of the village to such occasions. Indeed, on this particular evening, practically the entire local youth population could be seen making its way to the ship's gangplank.

Upon coming aboard, like any first-time visitors, they immediately set about taking a look around the whole ship to see what they could see. After touring the main, middle and upper decks, they ended up congregating in the restaurant and bar. The female contingent, as a rule, took to dancing, while the male half preferred drinking. The unusual circumstance of being on a ship plus the music and alcohol always engendered a state of excitement, occasionally making big trouble for the crew. Almost always there was not enough time, and the party-goers made a collective appeal to extend the festivities just a bit longer — say, by half an hour, and then more and more into the night.

On this particular occasion I was alone in my cabin, listening to the music wafting up from the restaurant, and attempting to make modifications to the convoy's schedule for the remainder of the trip. All at once I felt myself being stared at. I turned around and glimpsed her eyes on the other side of the window glass. That was nothing unusual — visitors often liked looking into the ship's cabins.

I got up and opened the window. She didn't go away. She continued looking at me with some embarrassment. I felt I wanted to do something for this woman standing alone on the deck just outside my cabin. I wondered why she wasn't dancing like the others — perhaps she was somehow unhappy? I offered to show her around the ship, and she silently nodded. I took her all over the ship, showed her the main office — which frequently impressed visitors with its elegant appointments: the rug covering the floor, the soft leather furniture, the computers. Then I invited her into my cabin, which consisted of a study-cum-sleeping-quarters and a carpeted reception room equipped with fine furniture, TV and VCR. I was probably most delighted at the time to impress a poor country girl with the achievements of our civilised world.

I opened in front of her a box of candies, poured two glasses of champagne and, thinking to add the finishing touches to the impression, put on a videotape of Vika Tsyganova[1] singing "Love and death" (*Liubov i smert*). The videotape included a number of other songs performed by my favourite artists. She lightly touched the champagne glass to her lips, looked intently at me, and asked:

"It's a challenge, eh?"

I expected just about any kind of question except that one. The expedition had *indeed* turned out to be quite a challenge, what with the difficult navigation conditions on the river and the crew (mainly students from the marine academy) smoking pot and pilfering merchandise from the store. We were frequently behind schedule and couldn't get to our planned stops on time where our arrival had been advertised in advance. These burdens and other worries often deprived me of the opportunity not only to admire the landscape along the river but even to get a normal sleep.

I muttered something meaningless to her — something like, "Never mind, we'll get through!", then turned toward the window and polished off my glass of champagne.

---

[1]*Viktoria (Vika) Tsyganova (née Zhukova)* — a popular Russian singer born 1963 in Khabarovsk in the Russian Far East. Her singing and stage career began in the mid-1980s. Since then she has produced numerous albums. The song "Love and death" was recorded in 1994.

We went on talking about this, that or the other, listening to the videotape in the background. We talked right up until the ship docked once more at the end of the party cruise. Then I escorted her to the gangplank. Upon returning to my cabin, I made a mental note: there was something very strange and unusual about this woman, and I was left with an unexpected feeling of lightness and brightness after talking with her. That night I had my first good sleep in many days. At long last I understood why: the woman on the ship had been Anastasia.

"So that was you, Anastasia?!"

"Yes. There, in your cabin, I memorised all the songs which I later sang to you in the forest. They were playing while we were talking. You see how simple it all is?"

"How did you happen to come on board?"

"I was interested in seeing what was going on, how you all lived. After all, Vladimir, I had been spending my whole time just taking care of dachniks.

"That day I had hurried to the village, sold the dried mushrooms which the squirrels had collected, and bought a ticket to your party cruise. Now I know a lot more about the class of people you call entrepreneurs. And I know you pretty well too.

"I feel I owe you a huge apology. I did not know how things would turn out, that I would be so drastically altering your future. Only I can no longer do anything about it, since *they* have seen to the fulfilment of this plan, and *they* are answerable only to God. For a time now you and your family will have great difficulties and challenges to overcome, but then that will all pass."

Still not understanding what Anastasia was specifically talking about, I intuitively felt that something was about to unfold itself to me that would go way beyond the usual parameters of our existence, something directly concerning me.

I asked Anastasia to tell me in more detail what she meant by altering my destiny, and "challenges". Listening to her at the time, I simply could not imagine how accurately her predictions would soon start being realised in real life. She continued her recounting, once more bringing me back to events of the past year.

"Back then, on the ship," she said, "you showed me everything, even your cabin, treated me to candies, offered me champagne, and then escorted me to the gangplank, but I did not leave the riverbank right away. I stood on the shore near some bushes, and I could see through the lighted windows of the bar how the young people of the village were still dancing and having a good time.

"You showed me everything, but you did not take me to the bar. I guessed why — I was not appropriately dressed, my head was covered in a shawl, my cardigan was not stylish, my skirt was too long. But I could take off the shawl. My cardigan was neat and clean, and I had pressed my skirt carefully with my hands before I came to see you."

I really *hadn't* taken Anastasia to the bar that evening on account of her rather strange clothes, beneath which, as it was now clear, this young girl had been hiding her remarkable beauty — something that immediately set her apart from everyone else. And I said to her:

"Anastasia, why would you have wanted to go to the bar? Do you mean you would have gone dancing there in your galoshes? Anyway, how would you know what dances young people do today?"

"I was not wearing galoshes at the time. When I exchanged my mushrooms for money to buy a ticket to your ship, I also bought a pair of shoes from the same woman. Granted, they were old shoes, and were tight on me, but I cleaned them with grass. As for dancing, all I would need is a one-time look, and that would be it. And what a dancer I'd be!"

"You were, I suppose, offended at me that night?"

"I was not offended. But if you had taken me to the bar, I do not know whether that would have been a good or a bad thing, but events might have turned out differently, and all this might not have happened. But I do not now regret that things happened the way they did."

"So *what* happened? What happened that night that was so terrible?"

"After you escorted me off the ship, you did not return right away to your cabin. First you dropped in to see the captain, and then the two of you headed for the bar. For you that was a normal thing to do. The moment you entered you both made an impression on the public. The captain looked prim and proper in his uniform. You were very elegant and gave a most respectable appearance. You were known to many in this village — the famous Megre. The owner of a

convoy of ships unique in these parts. And you fully realised that you
were making an impression.

"You sat down at a table with three young country girls. They were
all only eighteen years old, just out of school.

"The waiters immediately brought champagne, candies and new
wine-glasses to your table — prettier than the ones that were there
before. You took one of the girls by the hand, bent over and started
whispering something in her ear... compliments, I understand they
are called. Then you danced with her several times and the conversation continued. The girl's eyes were radiant, as if she were in another
world, a fairy-tale world. You took the girl out on deck, and gave her
a tour of the ship, just as you had me. You took her into your cabin
and treated her to champagne and candies just like me. But there
was something a little different in the way you behaved with this
young girl. You were in a cheerful mood. With me you were serious
and even morose, but with her you were cheerful. I could see all that
very well through the lighted window of your cabin and, possibly, I
felt a little as though I wanted to be there in the place of that girl."

"You don't mean to tell me you were jealous, Anastasia?"

"I do not know, it was somehow an unfamiliar feeling for me."

I recalled that evening and these young country girls who were
trying so hard to look older and more modern.

The next morning Captain Senchenko[2] and I once again had a
laugh at their night-time antics on the dock. Then in my cabin I realised that this girl was in such a state that she was ready to go to any
lengths... but I didn't have any thought about wanting to possess her.
I told Anastasia about this, and she replied:

"Still, you had stolen her heart. The two of you went out on deck,
it was drizzling, and you threw your jacket over the girl's shoulders.
Then you took her back to the bar."

"What were you doing, Anastasia, standing the whole time in the
bushes in the rain?"

---

[2] *Alexander Ivanovich Senchenko* — former captain of the *Patrice Lumumba,* now employed with the State River Transport Inspection Agency. Captain Senchenko was
qualified to navigate not only the river, but Obsk Bight, where the Ob flows into the
Karsk Sea.

"That was nothing. The drizzle was good and caressing. Only it interfered with my view. And I did not want my skirt and shawl to get wet. They were my mother's. My mother left them to me. But I was very lucky. I found a cellophane bag on the shore. I took off my skirt and shawl, put them in the bag and hid it under my cardigan."

"Anastasia, if you didn't go home and it started to rain, you should have come back to the ship."

"I could not have done that. You had already seen me off, and you had other concerns. Besides, everything was shutting down.

"When the party came to an end and the ship was due to depart, at the girls' request, especially the girl who was with you in your cabin, you delayed the departure. At that point everything was in your power, including their hearts, and you were intoxicated with this power. The young people of the village were grateful to the girls, and the girls too felt imbued with a sense of power, through you. They completely forgot about the young lads who were with them in the bar, guys they had been friends with in school.

"You and the captain escorted them to the gangplank. Then you went back to your cabin. The captain went up to the bridge, and then the signal sounded, and the ship slowly, very slowly began to pull away from the dock. The girl you had danced with stood on the shore beside her girlfriends and the young people who had waited around to see the ship off.

"Her heart was beating so strongly, it was almost trying to leap out of her breast and fly away. Her thoughts and feelings were all mixed up.

"Behind her back could be seen the outlines of the village houses with their darkened windows, while in front of her the sleek white steamship was departing for ever, illuminated with a host of lights, still abundantly pouring forth its music across the water and the night-time riverbank.

"The sleek white ship was where *you* were, after saying so many marvellous things to her she had never heard before, so charming and alluring.

"And all that was slowly distancing itself from her, for ever.

"Then she decided to do something in the sight of everyone. She squeezed her fingers into a fist and began shouting desperately:

'I love you, Vladimir!' And she did it again, and again. Did you hear her shouting?"

"Yes," I replied.

"You could not help hearing her, and members of your crew heard her too. Some of them went out on deck and began laughing at the girl.

"I did not want them to laugh at the girl. Then they stopped laughing, as if they had suddenly come to their senses. But you did not come out on deck, and the ship continued slowly moving away. She thought you could not hear her, and she continued stubbornly crying out: 'I love you, Vladimir!'.

"Then some of her girlfriends joined in, and they all cried out together. I wondered what that feeling was like — *love,* which makes people lose control of themselves, or, perhaps, I wanted to help that girl, and so I shouted with them: 'I love you, Vladimir!'

"It seemed as though I had forgotten at that moment that it was not enough just to simply utter words — there definitely had to be behind them feelings, an awareness and trustworthiness of natural information.

"Now I know how strong that feeling is, and it is hardly subject to reason.

"The country girl later began to go into a slump and take to the bottle, and it was a challenge for me to help her. Now she is married and burdened down with everyday cares. And I have had to add her love to mine."

The story of the girl threw me a little off balance. Anastasia's account managed to resurrect that evening in my memory in full detail, and everything had really happened just as she said. It was very real.

Anastasia's unique declaration of love did not make any impression on me. After seeing her lifestyle and getting to know how she looked at the world, I saw her more and more as some unreal personage, even though she was sitting right beside me and I could simply reach out my hand and touch her. A consciousness accustomed to judge things by other criteria could not accept her as an existing reality. And while at the beginning of our encounter I *had* been attracted to her, she no longer aroused in me the emotions I once had. I asked:

"So, you think these new feelings appeared in you just by chance?"

"They are desirable, they are important," replied Anastasia. "They are pleasant even, but I wanted you to love me too. I realised that once you got to know me and my world a little more closely, you would not be able to accept me as a normal person — as simply Man. Perhaps you would even be afraid of me occasionally...

"And that is exactly what happened. I myself am to blame. I have made many mistakes. I was anxious, for some reason, all the time. I was in a hurry, and I did not have the time to explain everything to you as I should. Perhaps it all just turned out silly? Eh? Do I need to reform myself?"

And with those words her lips hinted at a sad smile. She touched her breast with her hand, and I at once remembered what had happened that morning when I was in the glade with Anastasia.

25

Bugs

That day I had decided to join in Anastasia's morning routine. Everything went fine at first — I stood under the tree and touched various little shoots. She told me about different herbs, and then I lay down beside her on the grass. We were both completely naked, but even I wasn't cold — that might have been, of course, due to my running through the forest with her. I was in a splendid mood. I felt a sense of lightness, and not just physically, but inside me as well.

It all started when I felt a pinching sensation on my thigh. I raised my head and saw a small army of bugs crawling along my thigh and lower leg — including ants, and some sort of beetle. I lifted my arm to swat them, but to no avail. Anastasia seized my arm in mid-air and held it, saying: "Do not touch them." Then she got up on her knees in front of me, bent over and pinned my other hand to the ground. I lay there as if crucified. I tried to free my arms, but couldn't — I felt that was an impossibility. Then I tried to jerk myself free, with great effort. She kept restraining me, with very little effort, her smile never fading from her face. And still my body felt more and more crawling things, all tickling, biting and pinching, and I came to the conclusion that they were starting to eat me alive.

I was in her hands both literally and figuratively. Taking stock of the situation, I realised that nobody knew where I was, nobody would come here looking for me, and if they should happen to wander by, they would see my picked-over bones (indeed, if they saw any bones at all). And all sorts of things flashed through my head at that moment, and this was no doubt the reason my instinct for self-preservation kicked in, dictating the only feasible course of action in the situation. In desperation I sunk my teeth with all my might into Anastasia's bare breast, at the same time jerking my head from side to side. Upon hearing her scream I immediately loosened my grip on her breast. Anastasia loosened *her* hold, jumped up, one hand holding her breast, the other stretched upward, waving. She tried to smile. I too jumped up and shouted at her, feverishly brushing the crawling things off my leg.

"You wanted to feed me to those vermin, you forest witch! Well, I don't give in that easily!"

She continued waving and responding with a forced smile to the elements of Nature around her, which had begun reacting warily to her situation. Anastasia looked at me and slowly — not with her usual spritely gait — walked toward the lake, her head bowed. I kept standing in the same spot for some time, thinking what I should do next — return to the riverbank? But how would I find the way? Follow Anastasia, but what would be the point? Nevertheless, I headed for the lakeshore.

Anastasia was sitting on the shore, rubbing tufts of grass between the palms of her hands and dabbing its juice on that part of her breast where a huge bruise left by my bite was clearly visible. It was probably very painful for her. But what had been her thought in attempting to restrain me? I hovered around her for a little while before asking:

"Does it hurt?"

Without turning her head, she replied:

"It hurts more inside." And she silently continued rubbing in the juice from the tufts of grass.

"Why were you thinking to play tricks on me?"

"I was trying to be helpful. The pores of your skin are all plugged up, they cannot breathe. The little bugs would have cleaned them out. It is not that painful — in fact it is rather pleasant."

"And the snake I saw, wouldn't it have stung me in the leg?"

"It was not doing you any harm. Even if it had released its venom, it would have been only on the surface, and I would have rubbed it in at once.[1] The skin and muscles on your heel are deteriorating."

---

[1] *rubbed it in* — It should be noted that ointments with snake's venom are used for skin and muscle disorders. Contrary to popular belief, the venom of the vast majority of snakes is only *slightly* toxic for humans. As long as it does not penetrate into the blood-stream all at once, but gradually through the skin and muscular tissue, the concentration of poison in the blood never reaches dangerous levels.

"That's on account of a car accident," I said.

For a time neither of us spoke. The whole situation felt rather silly. Not really knowing what to say, I asked her:

"What happened? Why did not that invisible someone help you again, as before, when I lost consciousness?"

"The reason he did not help, was that I was smiling. And when you began biting me, I tried to smile."

I began to feel uncomfortable in her presence. Picking up a tuft of grass, I rubbed it between my hands as hard as I could, then knelt down in front of her and began dabbing her bruise with my moistened palms.

26

Dreams —
creating the future

Now that I have learnt more about Anastasia's feelings, about her desire to show, in spite of all her extraordinary traits, that she is still Man — a normal, natural human being, I realised what mental anguish I had caused her that morning. Once again I apologised to her. Anastasia responded that she wasn't angry, but now, after what she had done, she was afraid for me.

"What could you have possibly done that could be so frightful?" I asked, and once again I heard for the umpteenth time a story nobody should put forward seriously if they expect to be considered as normal as all the other people in our society. Nobody talks that way about themselves.

"When the ship left," Anastasia went on, "and the young people headed back to the village, I stood for a while all by myself on the riverbank, and I felt good. Then I ran off to my forest. The day passed as usual, but in the evening, when the stars had already come out, I lay down on the grass and began dreaming, and then worked out this plan."

"What kind of plan?"

"You see, the things that I know are partially known by various people of the world you live in. Collectively they know practically everything, only they do not fully understand how it works. Then I went and fancied how you will go to a large city and tell many people about me and my explanations. You will do this using the same methods by which you usually spread any kind of information: you will write a book. A great many people will read it and the truth will unfold to them. They will have fewer ailments, they will change their attitude toward children and work out a whole new way of educating them. People will become more loving, and the Earth will begin to emit more radiant energy. Artists will paint my portrait, and each portrait will be their very best masterpiece. I shall try to inspire them. They will make what you call a movie, and it will be the grandest film ever made. You will look at all this and remember me. You will meet wise people who will understand and appreciate what I told you, and they will explain a lot of things to you.

"You will trust their word more than mine, and realise that I am not a witch but actually Man, a human being. It is just that I have more information inside me than other people. What you write will be of tremendous interest, and you will become rich. You will have money in the banks of nineteen countries, and you will visit holy places and cleanse yourself of all the darkness that is in you. You will remember me and begin to love me, you will have the desire to see me again and to see your son. You will desire to become worthy of your son.

"My dream was so clear, but possibly a bit pleading, too. That is probably why everything happened the way it did. *They* took it as a plan of action and decided to carry people through the dark forces' window of time. That is permitted if the plan is formulated in detail on the Earth, in the heart and mind of an individual Man, an Earth dweller. No doubt *they* took this as a grandiose plan, perhaps they added something themselves, and this is why the forces of darkness have been hard at work of late. They have never been this active before. I realised this from the ringing cedar. Its ray has become a lot more powerful lately. And the ringing has got louder — the cedar is hurrying to give back its light and its energy."

As I listened to Anastasia, I began thinking more and more that she was utterly crazy, that maybe she had long ago escaped from some asylum and was living here in the forest, and here I had gone and slept with her! And now she might have a child. What a tale, indeed! Still, seeing how serious and concerned she was as she talked with me, I tried to calm her down.

"Don't you worry, Anastasia! Your plan is obviously unrealisable, and so there's no need for the forces of darkness and light to fight each other. You don't have a detailed enough knowledge about our everyday life, its laws and conventions. The thing is that an awful lot of books are being published right now, but, for some reason, even the works of well-known authors aren't selling. I'm no writer, and so I don't have either the talent or ability or education to write anything."

"That is correct. You did not have these things earlier, but now you do," she declared in response.

"Okay," I kept trying to assuage her fears, "even if I tried, nobody would print it, or believe in your existence."

"But I do exist. I exist for those for whom I exist. They will believe and help you just as I shall later help them. And together with those people we..."

I couldn't make sense of what she was saying right off, and once more I made an effort to calm her down:

"I shan't even make an attempt to write anything. There's absolutely no sense in it, don't you get it?"

"Believe me, you shall. *They* have already created a whole network of circumstances that will make you do this."

"What am I, think you — a puppet in somebody's hands?"

"And so much depends on you. But the forces of darkness will try to stop you with all the tricks in their arsenal. They will even try to drive you to suicide by creating an illusion of hopelessness."

"Enough, Anastasia! That's it! I'm sick and tired of listening to your fantasies."

"You think they are just fantasies?"

"Yeah, yeah, fantasies!" And I stopped short. It began to dawn on me as I calculated the timing in my head, and I understood. Everything Anastasia told me about her dreams, about our son, she had thought up last year, long before I knew her as well as I do now, long before I slept with her. Now, a year later, it was coming to pass.

"So, that means it's already coming to pass?" I asked her.

"Of course. If it had not been for *them* — and for me too, a little — your second expedition would not have been possible. After all, you were scarcely able to make ends meet after the first one, and you did not even have any claim to the ship."

"You mean to say you influenced the shipping line and the firms that helped me?"

"Yes."

"So you drove me to ruin and inflicted damage on them. What right have you to interfere like that? And here I've left the ship behind and am sitting here with you. Maybe right now everything's going to pieces back there. You've probably got some kind of hypnotic ability. No, worse than that, you're a witch, and that's it. Or a crazy hermit. You don't have anything — not even a house — and here you go philosophising in front of me, you sorcerer!

"I am an entrepreneur! Do you have any idea what that means? I'm an entrepreneur! Even if I am dying, my ships still ply the river, they bring goods to people. That's what I do — I bring things to people and I can give you any items you need. But what can you give me?"

"I? What can I give you? I can give you a drop of heavenly tenderness and I can give you rest. You will be a genius of bright-eyed cleverness. As your image I am blest."

"Image? Who needs your image? What sense can that express?"

"It will help you write the book for people."

"Oh, please! There you go again doing goodness-knows-what with that mysticism of yours! So, you can't just live like a normal person, are you sure?"

"I have never done anything bad to anyone and I never can. I am a human being! I am Man! If you are so concerned about earthly goods and money, just wait a little — it will all come back to you. I do owe you an apology for dreaming like that — dreaming that you will have a time of troubles, but for some reason I could think of no alternative back then. You do not see the logic, you need to be compelled to see it through the help of circumstances in your world."

"Excuse me!" I couldn't hold out any longer. "What's this about being 'compelled'? You do something like that, and you still want to be treated as a normal human being?!"

"I am Man, a human being, a woman!" Anastasia's agitation was clearly noticeable in her voice. "I only wanted, and I still only want, the good, I want only the light! I want you to be purified. That is why I thought back then about your trip to holy places, about the book. *They* have accepted this, and the forces of darkness are always fighting with them, but never have the dark forces scored a major victory."

"And what about you?" I countered. "With all your intelligence, information and energy, are you just going to stand and watch from the sidelines?"

"In a confrontation on this scale between two great principles my own efforts count for precious little — help is going to be needed from many others in your world. I shall seek them out and find them, just as I did that time when you were in hospital. Only you need to develop a little more of that conscious awareness. You need to overcome the bad within yourself."

"I'd like to know just what's so bad within myself — what did I do wrong when I was in hospital? And how could you have treated me when you weren't there beside me?"

"Back then you simply did not feel my presence, but I was right there with you. When you were on the ship, I brought you a little branch of the ringing cedar which Mama had broken off before she died. I left it in your cabin when you invited me in. You were ill even then. I could feel it. Do you remember the branch?"

"Yes," I replied. "In fact, that branch hung on the wall of my cabin for some time, many of my crew noticed it, and I brought it back to Novosibirsk. But I didn't pay any attention to it."

"You simply threw it out."

"But I had no idea..."

"No, you had no idea. You threw it out. And Mama's branch did not succeed in overcoming your illness. Then you went into hospital... When you get back, take a close look at the history of your illness. If you check the chart, you will see that in spite of taking the very best medicine available, there was no improvement.

"But then they gave you some cedar nut oil. Now, according to strict prescription regulations, the doctor was not supposed to do that, but she did it, in spite of the fact that there was not a single mention of it in your medical prescription guide and nothing of the sort had ever been done before. Do you remember?"

"Yes."

"You were being treated by a woman who is a sector head in one of the best clinics in your city. But this sector had nothing to do with your particular illness. She left you there, even though just one floor up there was another sector specifically corresponding to your illness — right?"

"Yes!"

"She would prick you with needles, and turn on some music in the half-darkened room."

Anastasia's account was in complete accord with what had actually happened to me.

"Do you remember this woman?"

"Yes. She was in charge of a sector in the former District Council hospital."[1]

And then all at once Anastasia, her eyes fixed intently on me, spoke several disconnected phrases which immediately shocked me and caused a shiver up and down my spine: "What kind of music do you like?... Fine... Like that? Not too loud?" And she spoke these phrases in exactly the voice and with the intonation used by the sector head who treated me.

"Anastasia!" I exclaimed.

She didn't let me finish.

"Keep listening. Do not be shocked, for God's sake. Do try... try to make sense of everything I am telling you. Get your mind-forces working, at least a little. It is all very easy, you see, for Man."

And she went on.

"This woman doctor — she is very good. She is a real doctor! I got along with her very well. She is kind and forthright. It was I who did not want you to be transferred to the other sector. That sector would have corresponded to your particular illness, but hers did not. She requested her supervisors to leave you with her, assuring them she would take care of you. She felt up to it. She knew your pains were simply the result of 'something else'. And she tried to counteract that 'something else'. She is a doctor!

"And how did you behave? You kept on smoking and drinking to your heart's content, eating salty and spicy foods, and that in spite of your serious ulcer. You did not deny yourself anything in the way of pleasure. Somehow your sub-conscious got a message, even though you were not aware of it, that there was nothing terribly wrong with you, that nothing would happen to you.

"I did not accomplish anything good — rather, the opposite. The darkness in your consciousness did not lessen, nor did your will or sense of awareness improve. When you regained your health, you sent one of your employees to thank the woman who saved your life.

[1] *District Council hospital* — this was a first-class hospital reserved (in Soviet times) for high-ranking Communist Party officials.

You yourself did not call her, not even once. She was waiting for you to call, she had such a feeling of love for you."

"She? Or you, Anastasia?"

"*We,* if that is clearer to you."

I got up and for some reason took a few steps away from Anastasia, who was sitting on a fallen tree. The mixed-up state of my feelings and thoughts caused even greater uncertainty as to how I should think about her.

"Now look, once again you are not understanding how I do things, you are becoming confused, but it is a simple thing to grasp — I do things with the help of my imagination and my ability to analyse possible situations. And now you have started thinking ill of me again."

She fell silent, her head resting on her knees. And I stood there too, without saying a word, thinking: She keeps on talking and talking and saying all sorts of incredible things. It's clear she has no idea that any normal person would not accept them, and so would not accept her as a normal person.

Still, I went over to Anastasia and brushed her cascading braids of hair from her face. Tears were rolling down her cheeks from her large bluish-grey eyes. She smiled and said something quite uncharacteristic:

"'She's just another one of those soppy females, eh?' Right now you are overwhelmed by the very fact of my existence and do not believe your eyes. You do not fully believe, and you cannot even make sense of my sitting here talking to you. You find both my existence and my abilities amazing. You have completely ceased accepting me as a normal human being, as Man. But believe me, I am a human being and not a witch.

"You consider my way of life amazing, but why does not a certain something else seem just as amazing, even paradoxical, to you? Why do people admit the Earth to be a celestial body, the greatest creation of the Supreme Mind with each system component as His greatest achievement, and then go tear this system apart and devote so much effort to its destruction?

"You see a manufactured space ship or aeroplane as something natural, in spite of the fact that all its components are made of broken or re-melted parts of the original supreme system.

"Imagine a being who breaks off a piece of an aeroplane in flight and uses its parts to make himself a hammer or a scraper, and then praises himself for having succeeded in making a primitive tool. He does not understand that one cannot keep breaking pieces off a flying aeroplane indefinitely.

"How can you not grasp that our Earth must not be tortured like that?...

"The computer is considered to be an achievement of the human mind, but few realise that the computer may simply be compared to a prosthesis of the brain.

"You can imagine what would happen to a person with normal, healthy legs if they walked on crutches all the time. Naturally, their leg muscles would atrophy.

"No machine will ever be superior to the human brain, provided the brain is kept in constant training."

Anastasia wiped away a tear rolling down her cheek and stubbornly persisted in elucidating the incredible revelations stemming from her extraordinary logic.

At the time I had no idea how everything she said would arouse millions of people, set the minds of scholars astir and, even as mere hypotheses, prove to be without parallel anywhere in the world.

According to Anastasia, the Sun is something like a mirror. It reflects emanations from the Earth which are invisible to the eye. These emanations come from people in a state of love, joy or some other radiant feeling. Reflecting off the Sun, they return to Earth in the form of sunlight and give life to everything on the planet.[2]

---

[2]Interestingly, the idea that Sun has no radiance of its own is in fact quite widespread in both science and religion. For example, a prominent Russian engineer and scientist living in France, Dr Georges Lakhovsky (1869-1942), a bioenergetics pioneer, author of *The secret of life: Cosmic rays and radiations of living beings* and one of the most respected European scientists of his time, has suggested that "The Sun is a cold black body". Viktor Schauberger (see footnote 1 in Chapter 16: "Flying saucers? Nothing extraordinary!") argued along the same lines, as discussed in Callum Coats's book *Living energies*. Dr Philip Callahan (1923-), a prominent entomologist and radio engineer, author of numerous scientific articles and books, speaks about *tachons*, particles travelling faster than the speed of light, and attempts to detect them in solar rays *and* around people in a state of love (e.g., saints or meditating yogis). George Ivanovich Gurdjieff (1872?-1949) was a spiritual thinker whose thought

She brought up a whole array of supporting arguments which were not that simple to grasp.

"If the Earth and other planets were simply consumers of the Sun's grace of light," she said, "it would be extinguished, or burn unevenly, and its glow would be off-kilter. In the Universe there is and can be no lopsided process. Everything is interrelated."

She cited, too, the words of the Bible: "And the life was the light of men".[3]

Anastasia also stated that one Man's feelings can be transmitted to another by reflecting off the celestial bodies, and she demonstrated this by the following example:

"Nobody on Earth can deny that you can feel when somebody loves you. This feeling is especially noticeable when you are with a person who loves you. You call it intuition. In fact, invisible light-waves emanate from the one who loves. But the love can be felt, if it is strong enough, even when the individual is absent. By drawing upon this feeling and understanding its nature, one can do wonders. This is what you call miracles, mysticism or incredible abilities. Tell me, Vladimir, do you not feel a bit better with me now? Somehow lighter, warmer, more fulfilled?"

"Yes," I replied. "For some reason I *have* started to feel warmer."

"Now watch what happens when I concentrate on you even more strongly."

Anastasia lowered her eyelids ever so slightly, slowly stepped back a few paces and stopped. A pleasant feeling of warmth started running through my body. It gradually intensified, but didn't burst into flame, and didn't make me hot. Anastasia turned and began to slowly walk away, hiding behind the thick trunk of a tall tree. The sensation of pleasant warmth did not lessen, and to it was added

---

had a profound influence on such prominent intellectuals of the twentieth century as naturalist Aldo Leopold (1887-1948), originator of land ethics and author of *A Sand County almanac*, and economist E.F. Schumacher (1911-1977), author of *Small is beautiful: Economics as if people mattered*. Gurdjieff maintained that Sun "neither shines nor warms" and devoted an entire chapter in his *Beelzebub's tales to his grandson* to a discussion of this seemingly paradoxical proposition.

[3]John 1: 4 (*Authorised King James Version*).

another — as though something were helping my heart pump blood through my veins, and with every heartbeat came the impression that the blood-streams were instantly reaching every little vein in my body. The soles of my feet broke out into a heavy sweat and became very moist.

"You see? Now is it all clear to you?" Anastasia said as she triumphantly re-appeared from behind the tree, confident that she had proved something to me. "You see, you felt all that when I went behind the tree-trunk, and your sensations even increased when you could not see me. Tell me about them."

I told her, and then asked in turn:

"What does the tree-trunk show?"

"What do you think? The waves of information and light went directly from me to you. When I hid myself, the tree-trunk was supposed to significantly distort them, since it has its own information and its own glow, but this did not happen. The waves of feelings began falling directly upon you, reflecting off the celestial bodies, and even intensified. Then I caused what you call a 'miracle' — your feet began to perspire. You failed to mention that fact."

"I didn't think it was important. How do my feet perspiring constitute a miracle?"

"I chased all sorts of diseases out your body through your feet. You should feel a lot better now. It is even noticeable on the outside — you are not slouching as much."

Indeed, I *was* feeling better physically.

"So, when you concentrate like that, you dream up something and whatever you want comes to pass?"

"That describes it, more or less."

"And does what you dream about always come to pass — even when you're asking for something besides bodily healing?"

"Always. As long as it is not an abstract dream. As long as it is detailed down to the minutest aspects and does not contradict the laws of spiritual being. I do not always manage, however, to come up with a dream like that. Thought has to proceed extremely quickly and there must be a corresponding vibration of feelings, and then it will definitely come true. It is a very natural process. It happens in the lives of many people. Ask around among your acquaintances.

Perhaps you will find some among them who have dreamt this way, and their dream has come true either fully or partially."

"Detailed... thinking... proceeding extremely quickly... Tell me, when you were dreaming about the poets and artists and the book, was that all in detail too? Did your thought proceed quickly then?"

"Extraordinarily quickly. And everything was so specific, down to the finest detail."

"So now, you think, it's going to come true?"

"Yes, it will."

"There wasn't anything else you dreamt about at the time? You've told me everything about your dreams?"

"Not everything."

"Then tell me everything."

"Do you... do you really want to hear it, Vladimir? Really?"

"Yes."

Anastasia's face brightened, as though illuminated by a flash of light.

It was with inspiration and excitement that she continued her incredible monologue.

27

Across the dark forces' window of time

"During that night of my dreams I thought of how to transport people across this window of time of the dark forces. My plan and conscious awareness were precise and realistic, and *they* accepted them.

"In the book you are going to write there will be unobtrusive combinations, formulations made up of letters, and they will arouse in the majority of people good and radiant feelings. These feelings are capable of overcoming ailments of body and soul, and will facilitate the birth of a new awareness inherent in people of the future. Believe me, Vladimir, this is not mysticism — it is in accord with the laws of the Universe.

"It is all very simple: you will write this book, guided only by feelings and your heart. You will not be able to do otherwise, since you have not mastered the technique of writing, but through your feelings you can do *anything*. These feelings are already within you. Both mine and yours. They are not something you can comprehend just yet. But they will be understandable to many. When they are embodied in signs and patterns, they will be stronger than Zoroaster's fire.[1] Do not hide anything that has happened to you, even your most intimate experiences. Free yourself from any sense of shame and do not be afraid of appearing ridiculous. Humble your pride.

"I have opened my whole being to you — my body and my soul. Through you I want to open myself to everyone. Now I am permitted to do this. I know what a terrible mass of dark forces will descend upon me, they will try to counteract my dream, but I am not afraid of them. I am stronger and I will succeed in seeing my plan

---

[1]*Zoroaster* (ca. 628–551 B.C.) — a Persian mystic, also known as *Zarathustra,* who compared the nature of God to an eternal, uncontainable flame. Zoroastrianism is practised today principally in India (where adherents are known as *Parsees*) and in isolated areas of Iran.

come true, and I will succeed in giving birth and raising my son. Our son, Vladimir.

"My dream will break down many of the devices of the forces of darkness, which for millennia have been acting on people destructively, and it will cause many to work for good.

"I know that you find yourself unable to believe me at the moment — you are prevented from doing this by the conventions and many dogmas planted in your brain by the circumstances of existence in the world in which you live. The possibility of transport through time seems incredible to you. But your concepts of time and distance are all relative. These dimensions cannot be measured by metres or seconds, but by the degree of one's conscious awareness and will.

"The purity of the thoughts, feelings and perceptions held by the majority is what determines the place of humanity in time and the Universe.

"You believe in horoscopes, you believe in your complete dependence on the position of the planets. This belief has been attained through the aid of the devices of the dark forces. This belief is slowing down the movement of the channel of light, allowing its dark counterpart to advance and increase in size. This belief is leading you away from a conscious awareness of the truth, the essence of your earthly being. Analyse this question very carefully. Think about how God created Man in His image and likeness.[2] Man has been granted great freedom — the freedom to choose between the darkness and the light. Man has been given a soul. The whole visible world is subject to Man, and Man is free even when it comes to his relationship to God — to love Him or not to love Him. Nobody and nothing can control Man apart from his own will. God wants Man's love in return for His love, but God wants the love of a free Man, perfect in His likeness.

"God has created everything we can see, including the planets. They serve to guarantee the order and harmony of all life — not only plants and animals, they also help human flesh, but there is no way they have power over Man's heart and mind. It is not they who

[2] *His image and likeness* — see Gen. 1: 26, 27.

control Man, but Man controls *their* movements through his subconscious.

"If a single individual wanted a second sun to flare up in the sky, it would not appear. Things are arranged this way so that planetary catastrophes do not happen. But if everybody together wanted a second sun, it would appear.

"In making up a horoscope, it is necessary first of all to take into account the basic dimensions — the level of Man's temporal awareness, his strength of will and his spirit, the aspirations of his soul and the degree to which it participates in the life of the here and now.

"Favourable and unfavourable weather, magnetic storms, high and low pressure — these are all subject to will and conscious awareness.

"Have you never seen a happy and joyful person on a cloudy or stormy day — or, on the other hand, a sad and depressed person on a sunny day amidst the most favourable weather conditions?

"You think that I am simply indulging in a crazy person's fantasy when I say that the patterns and formulations of letters I shall put in the book will heal people and illuminate their experience. You do not believe me because you do not understand. And yet in fact it is so simple.

"You see, right now I am talking to you in your language, using your speech idioms, and I even try sometimes to speak with your voice inflections. It will be easy for you to memorise what I say, because this is *your* language, belonging exclusively to you, although understandable to many people. It contains no incomprehensible words or obscure idioms. It is simple and therefore understandable to the majority. But there are certain words, or word orders, which I have changed, just a little — but only a little. Right now you are in an excited state and therefore, whenever you recall this state, you will recall everything I have told you. And you will write down what I have said.

"And that is how my combinations of letters will fall into place in your book.

"These combinations are very important. They can do wonders, just like prayer. After all, many of you already know that prayers are specific combinations and specific patterns of letters. These combinations and patterns are strung together, with God's help, by people who have had an illuminating experience.

"The forces of darkness have always tried to deprive Man of the opportunity of drawing upon the grace emanating from these combinations. To this end they have even changed the language, introduced new words and removed old ones, and distorted the meaning of words.

"At one time, for example, there were forty-seven letters in your language. Now there remain thirty-three alone. The forces of darkness have imported other combinations and fashions of their own, stirring up base and dark elements, attempting to lead Man astray by fleshly lusts and passions. But I have restored the original combinations using only the letters and symbols in use today, and they will now be effective. I tried so hard to find them... and I did! I have brought together all the best from different times. I collected a good many, and have hidden them in the lines that you will write.

"As you can see, it is simply a matter of translating the combinations of signs from the depth of eternity and infinity of the Universe — exact in sense, meaning and purpose.

"Write about everything you have seen, hold back nothing — neither the bad nor the good, nor even the intimate or absurd — and then they will be preserved.

"You yourself will be convinced of this, please believe me, Vladimir. You will become convinced once it is written down. In many who read what has been written, feelings and emotions will be found which they are not yet able to fully understand or make sense of. They will confirm this for you — you will see and hear it confirmed. And radiant feelings will appear in them, and then many will themselves understand, through the help of these feelings, a great deal more than what is written by your hand.

"Try writing at least a little. When you are convinced that people feel these combinations, when a dozen, or a hundred, or a thousand people confirm it for you, you will then believe and write down everything. Only believe. Believe in yourself. Believe in me.

"Later I can tell you things even more significant, and people will understand and feel them too. I am talking about the raising of children. You were interested to know about flying saucers and how they work, rockets and planets. But I so wanted to tell you more about the raising of children, and I shall do so. I shall explain it when I instil in you a greater sense of conscious awareness.

"However, all this needs to be read when there is no interference from sounds of manufactured, artificial devices around. Such sounds are harmful and lead Man away from the truth. Let only the sounds of the God-created natural world be heard. They carry within themselves truthful information and grace, and increase one's conscious awareness. Then the healing effect will be significantly more powerful.

"Once again, of course, you have your doubts when you think of me, and do not believe in the healing power of words. But there is no mysticism here — no mere fantasy or contradiction of the laws of spiritual being.

"When these radiant feelings appear in Man, they cannot help but exert a beneficial influence on literally every organ of his body. It is these radiant feelings that are the most powerful and effective remedy against any kind of bodily complaint. God has healed through the help of such feelings, as did the Biblical prophets and saints. Read the Old Testament and see for yourself. Certain people in your world are healing through the help of these feelings. Many of your doctors know about this. Ask them if you do not believe me. After all, it is easier for you to believe them. The stronger and brighter the feeling, the greater effect it has on the person in need of healing.

"I have always been able to heal with my ray. Great-Grandfather taught me and explained everything when I was still a child. I have done this many times with my dachniks.

"Now my ray is many times more powerful than Grandfather's and Great-Grandfather's. That is because, they say, there has arisen in me another feeling, the one called love.

"This feeling is so great, so pleasant, and a little fiery too. I want to share it with everyone, and with you. As for me, I want things to be good for everyone and everything, just as God wanted them to be."

Anastasia spoke her monologue with extraordinary inspiration and confidence, as though aiming it across space and time. And then she fell silent. I looked at Anastasia, amazed by her uncharacteristic fervour and confidence, and then asked:

"Anastasia, is that it? Are there no further nuances in your plans or dreams?"

"The rest, Vladimir, is just trifles, nothing of great significance. I merely included them — little things as simple as *ABC* — as I was formulating the plan. There was just one sticking point, concerning you, but I managed to resolve it."

"Well, please go into a bit more detail here. What kind of sticking-point was it, that concerned me?"

"You see, I made you into the richest person on earth. And I also made you the most famous. This will happen in the near future. But when the details of my dream unfolded... As yet it had not taken off, so to speak, it had not yet been taken up by the forces of light. The forces of darkness — they are always trying to inject their own harmful input, like all sorts of side effects, exerting a destructive influence on the person at the centre of the dream, and on other people too.

"My thoughts were dashing along ever so quickly, but the forces of darkness were still keeping pace. They had left many of their other earthly affairs in their attempts to concentrate their devices on my dream. But then I came up with something. I outwitted them. And I caused all their devices to turn about and work for the good. The forces of darkness lost their bearings for less than a split second, but that was enough for my dream to be snatched up by the forces of light and transported into radiant infinity, well beyond their sight and reach."

"And just what did you come up with, Anastasia?"

"Unexpectedly for them, I extended, just by a little, the dark forces' window of time — the time you will need to meet the various challenges. In doing so I deprived myself of the possibility of using my ray to help you. They were confounded, failing to see any logic on my part. And during this moment I very quickly shone my light on people who will be in touch with you in the future."

"And what does all this mean?"

"People will help you, will help realise my dream. They will do this with little rays of their own, which will be almost uncontrollable. But there will be a lot of them, and together you will make the dream come true in physical reality. You will be carried *across* the dark forces' window of time. And you will carry others with you.

"And becoming rich and famous will not make you greedy or arrogant. Because you will understand that money is not the point — it will never buy you the warmth or the genuine compassion of the human soul.

"You will understand this when you make your way across that window of time, when you see and get to know these people. And they too will understand. As for the deep knee-bends... This kind of relationship with the banks is something I also thought up because you are altogether negligent in taking care of your body. At least you will be getting some exercise whenever you withdraw money from your account. Some of the bank officials will do it, besides. And never mind if it looks a little funny. It means you will find yourself free from the sin of pride.

"So it has turned out that all these challenges and trials which the forces of darkness have concocted in their window of time will serve to strengthen you and those around you. All this will increase your sense of conscious awareness. And it will ultimately save you from the dark temptations they are so proud of. Their own actions will save you. This is why they lost their bearings for a split second! Now they will never be able to catch up to my dream!"

"Anastasia! My dear, precious dreamer! My fantasy-maker!"

"Oh... How good of you to say that! Thank you! Thank you! It was so good of you to say 'My dear'!"

"You're welcome. But, you see, I also called you a fantasy-maker. A dreamer. You're not offended?"

"Not at all. You do not know yet, how accurately my dreams always come true, when they turn out so clearly and in such detail. This one will come true without fail. It is my favourite dream, the clearest of them all. And the book you write will come into being, and people will start having extraordinary feelings, and these feelings will call people to action..."

"Wait, Anastasia! You're getting carried away again. Calm down."

Only a short time had gone by before my interruption of Anastasia's fervent stream of speech, which seemed indeed but a fantasy.

I couldn't quite grasp the significance behind this monologue of hers. Everything she said sounded *too* fantastic. Only a year later Mikhail Fyrnin,[3] editor of the magazine *Chudesa i prikliuchenia (Wonders and Adventures)*, after reading my manuscript containing this monologue, excitedly handed me the latest issue of his magazine — the issue of May 1996.

The contents of the magazine overwhelmed me with excitement. Two major scholars, both academicians, — Anatoly Akimov[4] and Vlail Kaznacheev[5] — talked in their articles about the existence of a Supreme Mind, the close interrelationship of Man and the Universe, as well as about certain rays, invisible to normal sight, emanating from Man. Scientists have now been able to identify them with special equipment, and the magazine included two photographs of these rays emanating from people.

But science has only begun to talk about what Anastasia has not only known from childhood, but has been applying in her daily life, in her endeavours to help others.

How was I to know a year earlier that this girl standing before me in an old skirt (the only one she possessed) and uncomfortable-looking galoshes, nervously picking at the buttons on her cardigan — this girl named *Anastasia* — actually possessed a vast store of knowledge as well as the ability to influence human destinies. Or that the pulse-beats of her soul are in fact capable of counteracting

---

[3]*Mikhail A. Fyrnin* — an editor with the publishing house *Molodaya gvardia (Young Guard)* for more than 25 years, where he worked in particular on a series entitled "Lives of remarkable people". One of his more recent major projects was the compilation of *Sobranie myslei Dostoevskogo (Collection of Dostoevsky's thoughts)*, published in Estonia in 2003.

[4]*Anatoly Evgenevich Akimov* — Director of the International Institute of Theoretical and Applied Physics of the Russian Academy of Natural Sciences.

[5]*Vlail Petrovich Kaznacheev* (1924–) — a prominent member of the Russian Academy of Medical Sciences from Novosibirsk, specialising in the interrelationship between Man and Nature, including bio-systems and information processes. A decorated World War II veteran, Dr Kaznacheev has received numerous awards for his research and publications.

the dark and destructive forces threatening mankind. Or that the well-known Russian healer Vladimir Mironov[6] would tell a gathering of his assistants that "We are all ants compared to her", adding that the world has not yet known a power greater than hers and regretting that even after spending such a long time with her I had still not understood her.

Many people were to feel the energy of a tremendous power emanating from the book.

Following the first small-scale printing of this book, for which I have to give credit to Anastasia herself as one author, would come a sprinkling of verses in abundance, washing away dirt like a spring rain.

Now, dear reader, this is the very book which you are holding in your hands and which you are reading at this moment. Whatever feelings it is arousing in your heart is for you alone to judge. What do you feel? What is it calling upon you to do?

Staying there alone in her glade in the taiga, Anastasia will use her ray of goodness to eliminate any barriers standing in the way of her dream. And she will gather and inspire more and more newcomers to make her dream come true.

And so, at my challenging moments three Moscow students[7] will come to my side and stand by me. They will not receive any significant compensation for their efforts and will even end up helping me financially. Earning their living wherever they can, they — especially Lyosha Novichkov — will spend nights keyboarding the *Anastasia* text into their computers.

They will not cease their keyboarding work, even after their difficult examination session begins.

And Moscow Printshop Number Eleven will put out a 2,000-copy print run. They'll do this on their own, by-passing a publishing house. But even before this, the journalist Evgenia Kvitko of the agricultural

---

[6]*Vladimir Andreevich Mironov* — a Doctor of Alternative Medicine, who runs his own natural therapy clinic in south-central Moscow, and has published several books and numerous articles on the subject.

[7]*three Moscow students* — the reference is to Alexey (Lyosha) Novichkov, Artem Semenov and Anton Nikolaikin, who will eventually support Vladimir in a number of ways in carrying out the provisions of Anastasia's plan (see Book 2 in the series).

paper *Krestyanskie vedomosti* will be the first to tell about Anastasia in the press. Later Ekaterina (Katya) Golovina from *Moskovskaya pravda,* and then *Lesnaya gazeta, Mir novostei* and Radio Rossiya. The magazine *Chudesa i prikliuchenia (Wonders and Adventures),* which publishes articles by the brightest lights of Russian academia, will throw tradition to the wind and devote several issues to Anastasia, explaining:

"In their boldest dreams our academics come nowhere near the insights of Anastasia, the wise woman of the Siberian taiga. Purity of thought makes Man omnipotent and omniscient. Man is the apex of creation."

Anastasia will be published only by the major press outlets in Moscow. Anastasia herself seems to have made that choice in preference to the tabloids, in a careful effort to preserve the purity of her dream.

But all this did not become clear to me until a year after my visit with her. Not understanding her at the time, and not fully believing, I had my own take on the experience, and tried to shift the conversation to a topic I was more familiar with — namely, entrepreneurs.

28

Strong people

The highest evaluation of your personality comes from those around you.

Anastasia talked a lot about the people we call entrepreneurs, about their influence on public spirituality, and then took a twig and drew a circle on the ground. Inside it she drew many little circles, with a dot in the middle of each one. Off to the side there were more circles. It was like a map of the planets around the Earth, and she kept adding still many more little circles inside, and said:

"The large circle is the Earth — a planet inhabited by people. The little circles are small groups of people, linked together into collectives. The dots are the people in charge of these collectives. The way these heads relate to the people in their group, what they make them do, what kind of psychological climate they create through their influence will determine whether the people around them fare well or poorly. If the majority fare well, a bright ray emanates from each of them and from the group as a whole. If poorly, then the ray is dark."

And Anastasia shaded in some of the circles, making them dark.

"Naturally, their inner state is influenced by many other factors as well, but in the space of time during which they are in this group, the principal thing is their interrelationship with the person in charge. For the Universe it is very important that a bright radiance should emanate from the Earth. The radiance of the light of love and good. This is mentioned in the Bible, as well: 'God is love'.[1]

"I feel sorry, very sorry, for the people you call entrepreneurs. They are the most miserable of all. I would so much like to help them, but it is difficult for me to do that all by myself."

---

[1]I John 4: 8 & 16 *(Authorised King James Version)*.

"You're mistaken, Anastasia. The most miserable people in our society are the pensioners, people who can't find work, can't afford a roof over their heads, or even food or clothing. An entrepreneur is someone who has all these things in greater abundance than other people. He has access to pleasures which others can't even dream about."

"What specifically, for example?"

"Well, even if you take the average entrepreneur, he will have a modern car and apartment. He will not have any problems with food and clothing."

"And what about joy? What does he find satisfaction in? Come and see for yourself."

Once again Anastasia led me to the grass and, like the first time, when she showed me the woman dachnik, she began to show me other scenes.

"You see? There he is, sitting right now in a car you would call pretty snazzy. You see — he's sitting alone in the back seat, and the car is air-conditioned — it has its own micro-climate, so to speak. His chauffeur is driving it very smoothly. But look and see how worried and pensive the entrepreneur sitting in the back seat is — he is thinking, working out plans, he is afraid of something. See — he has picked up what you call a telephone. He is upset... Yes, he has just received some news... Now he must quickly evaluate the situation and make a decision. He is all tensed up... Thinking. Now he is ready, the decision has been made. Now look, look — he appears to be sitting peacefully, but his face betrays doubt and concern. And there is no joy."

"That's *work*, Anastasia."

"That is a way of life, and there is no respite in it from the moment he wakes in the morning until the moment he goes to bed at night, or even in his sleep. And he sees neither the leaves unfolding on the trees nor the streams of spring.

"All around him are perennially envious onlookers, desiring to have what he has. His attempts to fence himself off from these by what you call bodyguards, a house — more of a citadel, actually — do not bring any complete sense of peace, since fear and worry have crept in and will forever remain with him.

"This goes on until his dying day, and just before the end of his life, he feels a sense of regret that he is obliged to leave it all behind."

"An entrepreneur has his joys," I observed. "They come when he obtains a desired result, or fulfils a plan he's thought up."

"Not true, Vladimir. He never gets to enjoy his acquisitions, since along comes another plan immediately to take its place — a more complicated plan, and the whole process begins again from scratch, only with greater challenges."

This forest princess painted me a rather sad and gloomy picture of our outwardly well-off social class, and this was not a picture I felt like accepting. I attempted a counter-argument:

"You forget, Anastasia, their ability to reach a set goal and obtain the good things in life, excited glances from women, respect by people around them."

To which she replied:

"Sheer illusion. There is nothing of the sort. Where have you ever seen a respectful or an excited glance directed at a passenger in a snazzy car or at the owner of the fanciest house in town? Not a single person will confirm what you have just said. These are but glances of envy, indifference and irritation. And even women cannot love these people, because their feeling is mixed in with their desire to possess not only the man but his property too. The men, in turn, cannot really love a woman, for there is no way they can free up enough room for such an important feeling."

It was useless to look for further arguments, since what she said could be confirmed or refuted only the people she was talking about. As an entrepreneur myself, I never really thought about what Anastasia was describing, never analysed how many minutes of joy I actually experienced, and most certainly could not do this for anyone else. For some reason it is simply not accepted in entrepreneurs' circles to whine or complain — everyone tries to show himself as successful and content with life.

This is no doubt why most people hold the stereotype image of the entrepreneur as someone who has received more than his share of good things in life. Anastasia was perceiving not the externally expressed feelings, but those which are more delicate and hidden in the inner recesses of one's heart. She was measuring a person's state of well-being by the amount of light she could detect in them. As to the scenes and situations she was able to see, I felt I was picturing them more from listening to her. I mentioned this to Anastasia, and she responded:

"I shall help you now. It is simple. Close your eyes, lie down on the grass, hands out to the sides, and relax. Picture in your mind the whole Earth, try to see its colour and the pale bluish glow emanating from it. Then narrow the focus of your imagination's ray so that it does not take in the whole Earth. Rather, make it narrower and narrower until you see concrete details. Look for people where the bluish light is stronger than in other places. Keep on narrowing your ray and you will eventually focus on one person, or a small group. Now try again, with my help."

She took me by the hand, ran her fingers along mine, resting her fingertips in my palm. The fingers of her other hand, which was lying on the grass, were pointed upward. I went through in my mind all the steps she outlined, and began to get a fuzzy image of three people sitting at a table engaged in a lively conversation. I couldn't understand what they were saying, as I wasn't picking up any voices at all.

"No," said Anastasia, "those are not entrepreneurs. Wait a moment, we shall find some."

She searched and searched with her ray, peering into offices both large and small, private clubs, party celebrations and bordellos... The bluish glow was either very weak or not there at all.

"Look — it is night-time here already, and this entrepreneur is sitting alone in a smoky office. Something is not right... But look at that one, how contented he looks, in a swimming pool, surrounded by pretty girls. He is tipsy, but there is no glow. He is simply trying to run away from something, his feeling of self-satisfaction is artificial...

"This one is at home. There is his wife, and his little one is asking him something... The telephone is ringing... You see there, he has become serious again, and pushed his family to the background..."

All sorts of situations became illuminated one after another, some of them outwardly good and some not so good... until we happened upon a most frightening scene. All at once appeared a room, probably in some apartment, quite nice-looking, but...

On a round table lay a naked man, his hands and feet tied to the table legs, his head hanging over, his mouth covered with brown sticky tape. At the table were sitting two burly-looking youths — one of them with a close-shaven head, the other with smooth, slick hair. A little distance away, under a floor lamp, there was a young woman in an arm-chair. Her mouth was also taped over, and she was tied to the chair with her linen sash bound tight around her waist. Both her legs were tied to the chair legs. She was wearing nothing but a torn undergarment. Next to her was sitting a thin, wiry man who was taking a drink of something, possibly cognac. On a small table in front of him lay a chocolate bar. The youths sitting at the round table weren't drinking. I could see them pouring some kind of liquid over the chest of the man lying on the table — vodka, or pure alcohol, and set it alight. A break-in, I surmised.

Anastasia shifted her ray away from this scene. But I cried out:

"Go back! Do something!"

She went back to the scene and replied:

"I cannot. It has already happened. This cannot be stopped now. It should have been stopped earlier, but now it is too late."

I watched spellbound and suddenly got a clear glimpse of the woman's eyes, filled with sheer horror and not even pleading for mercy.

"Do something!" I cried to Anastasia. "If you have any heart at all, do at least something!"

"It is not within my power. Everything has been, so to speak, programmed in advance, but not by me. I cannot interfere directly. They have the upper hand right now."

"But where's that goodness of yours — your powers?"

Anastasia didn't say a word. The horrifying scene began to blur a little. Then the older man who had been drinking the cognac suddenly disappeared.

All at once I felt a weakness throughout my body.

I could also feel the arm Anastasia was touching start to grow numb.

I could hear her somewhat weakened voice say, with evident difficulty in getting out the words:

"Take your hand away, Vladi—." She couldn't even finish saying my name.

I stood up, and drew my hand away.

My arm just hung there as if paralysed (as happens sometimes when you get a tingling sensation in your arms or legs) and went completely white. Then I wiggled my fingers a little and the numbness began to go away.

I looked at Anastasia in shock. Her eyes were closed. The blush had drained from her cheeks and it seemed as though there was not a drop of blood left under the skin on her hands and face.

She did not even seem to be breathing as she lay there. The grass for about three metres all around her had also become white and bent over. I realised something terrible had happened and cried out:

"Anastasia! What's happened to you, Anastasia?"

But there was not even the slightest response to my cry. Then I grabbed her by the shoulders and shook her body, which was no longer supple but had somehow gone limp. There was no response — her completely white, bloodless lips remained silent.

"Can you hear me, Anastasia?!"

She opened her eyelids ever so slightly and looked at me through her dimmed eyes, which had lost all their characteristic expression. I grabbed a flask of water, lifted up Anastasia's head and tried to give her something to drink, but she was unable to swallow. I looked at her, feverishly wondering what to do.

At long last she managed to move her lips just a tiny bit and to whisper:

"Carry me over there... to the tree."

I lifted her limp body and carried it out of the circle of whitened grass, and laid it down by the nearest cedar tree. In a little while she started to come round, and I asked:

"What happened to you, Anastasia?"

"I tried to fulfil your request," she quietly said, and a moment later added: "I think I succeeded."

"But you look so bad — you almost died!"

"I violated the natural laws. I interfered in something I should not have. That required all my strength and energy. I am surprised that they held out at all."

"Why did you take such a risk, if you knew it was so dangerous?"

"I had no choice. After all, you wanted me to do something. I was afraid that if I did not fulfil your request, you would lose all respect

for me. You would think that all I can do is talk, that I am all words...
And that I could not do anything in real life."

Her eyes looked at me enquiringly and pleadingly. Her soft voice
trembled a little as she spoke.

"But I cannot explain to you how to do it, how this natural system
works. I feel it, but I cannot explain to you in a way you could understand, and your scholars, probably, will not be able to explain it
either."

She bowed her head, fell silent for a while, as though mustering
her strength. Then she looked at me once more with pleading eyes
and said:

"Now you are going to be even more persuaded that I am abnormal, or a witch."

All at once I felt the tremendous urge to do something good for
her, but what? I wanted to tell her that I did consider her a normal
human being, a beautiful and intelligent woman, but in all honesty I
didn't feel about her the way I usually felt about women, and she with
that intuition of hers would not believe me.

And then I suddenly recalled her story about how her great-grandfather customarily greeted her as a child. About how this old grey-
haired fellow would stand on one knee before the little Anastasia and
kiss her hand. I got down on one knee before Anastasia, grasped
hold of her still pale and slightly cold hand, kissed it and said:

"If you are indeed abnormal, then you are the best, the kindest,
the cleverest and the most beautiful of all abnormal people ever!"

At long last a smile once more alighted upon Anastasia's lips, and
her eyes looked at me in gratitude. A rosy blush was coming back to
her cheeks.

"Anastasia, that was quite a depressing scene. Did you choose it
deliberately?"

"I was looking for something good, just as an example, but I could
not find anything. They are all held in the grip of their worries and
cares. They are constantly facing their problems all alone. They have
practically no spiritual communication."

"So what can be done? What can you suggest, apart from pitying
them? And I should tell you: these are strong people, these entrepreneurs."

"Very strong," she agreed, "and most interesting. It is as though they are living two lives in one. One life is known only to them and not even their family, while the other is the outward life, which people around them see. They can only be helped through increasing their sincere, spiritual communication with each other. They need to strive, with complete sincerity, for purity of thought."

"Anastasia, in all probability I shall try to do what you have asked. And I shall try to write a book, and establish an organisation of entrepreneurs with pure thoughts, but only in a way that I can understand."

"It will be difficult for you. I shall not be able to offer you sufficient help, I have little strength left. It will take a long time for my strength to recover. For a time I shall not be able to see at a distance with my ray. I am having difficulty seeing you right now with my ordinary eyesight."

"Don't tell me you're going blind, Anastasia!"

"I think it will all get better. Only it is a pity that for some time I shall not be able to help you."

"You don't need to help me, Anastasia. Just try to keep yourself for your son and help other people."

I needed to leave, to catch up to my ship. After waiting until she had started to regain her almost normal appearance, I got into the motorboat. Anastasia took hold of the bow with her hand and pushed the boat away from the shore. The boat was swept up and began floating downstream with the current.

Anastasia stood in the water almost up to her knees. The hem of her long skirt got wet and flapped about in the waves.

I gave the starting-cord a tug. The motor roared into life, breaking the silence I had grown accustomed to over the past three days. The boat gave a jerk forward, picked up more and more speed, and soon began to distance itself from the diminutive figure of the taiga recluse standing all alone in the shallow water near the riverbank.

All at once Anastasia rushed out of the water and started running along the bank after the boat.

Her long hair, trailing behind her from the headwind, looked like a comet's tail. She tried to run very fast, probably using up all her remaining strength in an effort to do the impossible — catch up to a speeding motorboat. But even *she* wasn't up to that. The distance between us gradually increased. I started feeling sorry for her fruitless efforts. Wanting to shorten the difficult moments of parting, I pushed down on the gas lever with all my might.

Then the thought flashed through my head that Anastasia might think that I had taken fright once more and was running away.

The motor, now roaring in bursts, lifted the boat's bow out of the water, making it speed forward faster and faster, and increasing the distance between us even more.

As for her... Oh Lord! What was she doing?

Anastasia ripped off the wet skirt that was slowing her down and cast aside her torn clothes. She increased her tempo, and the incredible happened: the distance between her and the boat gradually began to *decrease.*

On the path ahead of her loomed a steep slope, leading to an almost vertical drop-off. Continuing to press the gas lever to the limit, I thought that the incline would stop her in her tracks and bring this difficult episode to a quick end.

But Anastasia continued her headlong rush, occasionally stretching out her arms in front of her, as though using them to sense the space ahead.

Could it be that her eyesight had become so poor that she couldn't see the slope?

Without slowing down in the least, Anastasia ran straight up the slope. Reaching the top, she fell on her knees, threw up her arms toward the sky, turned slightly in my direction, and began shouting something. I could hear her voice over the wild roar of the motor and the noise of the waves. I heard as though in a whisper:

"There are sha-a-allows ahe-e-ad, sha-a-allows, su-u-unken lo-o-ogs!"

I quickly jerked my head forward, not fully able to grasp what was happening, and gave such a hard pull on the rudder that the lower side of the sharply tilted boat almost submerged to the point of taking on water.

A huge sunken log, one end grounded in a sandbar, the other barely visible on the surface, lightly scraped against the side of the speeding boat. If it had been a direct hit, it would easily have torn a gaping hole in the thin aluminium bottom.

Once out in mid-channel, I turned to glance at the cliff and whispered in the direction of the lonely figure standing on her knees, which was slowly being transformed into a vanishing dot:

"Thank you, Anastasia!"

29

Who are you, Anastasia?

The ship was waiting for me at Surgut.[1] The captain and crew were awaiting my instructions. But there was no way I could concentrate my efforts on working out the subsequent itinerary, and ordered the ship's crew to continue standing in port at Surgut, hold parties for the local population to come and have a good time, and keep up the promotion and sales exhibits.

My thoughts were occupied with my experiences with Anastasia. At a local shop I purchased a great deal of popular-science literature, books on extraordinary occurrences and people's unusual abilities, as well as the history of Siberia. I squirrelled myself away in my cabin, trying to find in all these books some sort of plausible explanation.

In addition, I wondered whether Anastasia's shouting of "I love you, Vladimir!" in her attempts to help the village girl could have really engendered in her a feeling of love for me.

How is it that mere words, which we often utter without putting a sufficient amount of suitable feeling into them, could have affected Anastasia — in spite of the differences in our ages and views on life and lifestyles?

The popular-science literature gave me no clues. Then I picked up the Bible. And there it was — my answer. At the very outset of the Gospel according to John I read: "In the beginning was the *Word,* and the *Word* was with God, and the *Word* was God."[2]

For the umpteenth time it struck me how laconic and precise were the definitions of this amazing book.

---

[1] *Surgut* — a city of 270,000 founded in the 16th century on the banks of the River Ob, which shares its proximity to the 60th parallel of latitude with St. Petersburg, Helsinki, Oslo, Churchill (Manitoba) and Whitehorse (Yukon). Surgut is a large centre of oil and gas industry.

[2] John 1: 1 *(Authorised King James Version).*

Immediately a lot of things became clearer in my mind. Anastasia, incapable as she was of trickery or deceit, could not just simply utter meaningless words. I remembered her saying:

"It seemed as though I had forgotten at that moment that it was not enough just to simply utter those words — there definitely had to be behind them feelings, an awareness and trustworthiness of natural information."[3]

O God!!! How disappointingly her hopes had turned out! Why had she addressed these words to me — here I was no longer in my prime, someone with a family, enslaved to a great many of this world's temptations, dark and destructive, as she herself said? With her degree of inner purity she deserves someone else entirely. But who could fall in love with her, given such an extraordinary lifestyle, mentality and intellect?

At first glance she comes across as an ordinary girl, albeit extremely beautiful and attractive. But once you get to know her it is as though she is transformed into some kind of creature living way beyond the bounds of the rational.

It may very well be that this impression of mine is due to my imperfect knowledge of things, my insufficient understanding of what constitutes our being. Others might have an entirely different perception of her.

I recalled that even at our parting I did not feel any particular desire to kiss or embrace her. I don't know whether she would have wanted me to or not. Anyway, what exactly did she want? I recalled her telling me of her dreams. What a strange philosophical bent her love had: organise a fellowship of entrepreneurs to help them? Write a book passing along her advice to people? Carry people across the dark forces' window of time?

And she believes it all! She is convinced that that's how it will all turn out. Oh, I was a good one — I promised I would try and organise a fellowship of entrepreneurs and write a book. Now she'll probably be having even more fantastic dreams about that. She might have thought up something simpler, more realistic.

[3]See Chapter 24: "A strange girl" above.

An inexplicable sense of pity for Anastasia arose in my heart. I could imagine her sitting there in her forest waiting and dreaming that everything would work out that way in broad daylight. Fine, if she were simply content to wait and dream. But, who knows, she may go beyond that and start taking steps on her own, focusing that ray of goodness of hers, expending the colossal energy of her heart and believing in the impossible. And even though she showed me what she could do with her ray and attempted to explain to me how it works, somehow my consciousness still can't accept it as something real. Judge for yourselves, dear readers — in her own words, she aims her ray at a person, illuminates this person, this Man, with an invisible light, and imparts to him her feelings and aspirations toward goodness and light.

"No, no, do not just think that I am interfering with a person's mental make-up, that I am violating his heart and mind," I remember her telling me. "Man is free — people are free — to accept or reject my advice. Only to the degree that they themselves find it to their liking, something close to their heart, will they be able to accept these feelings as their own. Then they will become lighter and brighter in their appearance too, and your diseases will leave them, either partially or completely. My grandfather and great-grandfather can do this, and I have always been able to — Great-Grandfather taught me, when he played with me in my childhood. But now my ray has become many times stronger than Grandfather's and Great-Grandfather's, because in me has been born that extraordinary feeling called love. It is so bright and clear, and even a little fiery. There is such a lot of it, and I want to share it."[4]

"With whom, Anastasia?" I had asked.

"With you, with others, with anyone who can accept it. I want everyone to experience good. When you begin to do what I have dreamt of, I shall bring many of these people to see you, and together you…"

Remembering all this, picturing her in my mind, I suddenly realised that I couldn't help but carry out — at least *try* to carry out her

[4]See Chapter 27: "Across the dark forces' window of time" above.

wishes. If I didn't, I would be tormented with doubt for the rest of my life, along with the feeling that I had betrayed Anastasia and her dream. Perhaps her dream wasn't all that realistic, but it was something she passionately desired.

I made my decision, and the ship headed full steam for Novosibirsk.

The unloading and disassembly of the exhibit equipment I left to my firm's executive director. After somehow managing to explain the situation to my wife, I set out for Moscow.

I set out for Moscow to make — or at least try to make — Anastasia's dream come true.

To be continued...

30

Author's message to readers

Dear readers, thank you. Thank you all who have responded to Anastasia with kindness and understanding. Indeed, I could not imagine that she would actually be capable of arousing so many feelings and emotions. I would so like to answer all your letters individually, but for the time being at least, this is physically impossible. The last lines of this book were penned in the Caucasus, where I have joined local archaeologists and enthusiasts in investigating the dolmens[1] Anastasia spoke about. And we found them. Saw them with our own eyes. Took pictures. These are ancient stone constructions, ten thousand years old. They have functional significance even for people living today.

They are located in the south, in the mountains of the Caucasus, not far from the cities of Novorossiysk, Gelendzhik and Tuapse.[2] They are the precursors of the pyramids of Egypt. But the local residents didn't pay any attention to the dolmens, not appreciating their purpose. Even though the dolmens were classified as historic monuments, they were ransacked by the local population. Their huge stones were carted off, and even used to build a church in the

---

[1] *dolmen* — a megalithic tomb (also known as a *portal tomb*) built of heavy upright stones (each weighing between 5,000 and 13,000 kg) with an even larger flat one on top and a small sealed entry portal at the front. While this specific type of tomb construction is unique to the north-western Caucasus, the term *dolmen* is also applied to megalithic configurations in Britain, Ireland, the Mediterranean and Northern Europe.

[2] *Novorossiysk* — port on the Black Sea in the Krasnodar region, with a population of just over 200,000, founded after the Russo-Turkish War of 1828–29; *Gelendzhik* — a resort town on the Black Sea about 45 km south-east of Novorossiysk, dating from the 1840s; *Tuapse* — a small port on the Black Sea just a few kilometres south-east of Gelendzhik, mentioned as early as the Byzantine chronicles of the 6th century B.C. (in the Greek variant: *Topsida*), although evidence of human life here is said to date back thousands of years.

settlement of Beregovoe,[3] which to me is nothing short of sheer blasphemy. Perhaps it was for this reason that forty priests were cruelly tortured to death in the Kuban region[4] during the revolutionary period of Russian history — one priest for each dolmen stone. People carried these stones off, not fully appreciating their significance.

Now that Anastasia has spoken about them, all this will change. It is amazing, but a fact: much of what she said has already been confirmed.

And even the fluctuations she talked about — the background radiation of the Earth fluctuating near the dolmens — have been detected and reported on by local health officials. Out of all the things Anastasia told or showed to me, I have decided to publish only what has been directly or indirectly corroborated by scientific experiments, material objects or historical facts.

Though I am starting to think that we'd better simply listen some more with our hearts. It would be quicker that way. The other method of confirmation takes up an awful lot of time. As with the dolmens, for example.

It took me pretty much half a year to collect historical data and trek through the Caucasus mountains to see the dolmens with my own eyes, and take pictures of them. I was, finally, convinced. But at the end of the day it turns out that if I'd simply believed right off, I could have used this half-year to greater advantage. It turns out that a great deal depends on one's ability to believe.

I did get a chance to visit Anastasia a second time. I got a chance to see the son she bore, and how she relates to him. A most unusual relationship. In addition, I had the opportunity of finding out from the people who ferried me to the spot on the riverbank about the various attempts on the part of both individuals and groups to penetrate Anastasia's domain and find her dwelling-place for themselves. Many, no doubt, wish to see and talk with her out of

[3]*Beregovoe* — a small outpost (*stanitsa*) located in a valley 5 km inland from the coast, 30 km to the south-east of Gelendzhik.

[4]*Kuban region* — the area of the Krasnodar region that forms the basin of the Kuban River in the north-western Caucasus.

well-meaning motives. But the people who ferried me also told me about a group of scoundrels who set up camp on the riverbank, sent out a helicopter to take pictures of the area, and tried to capture her. She was obliged to emerge from the taiga to talk with them and then send them packing, despite their attempts to restrain her physically. I shall tell all about that in the second book.[5]

I only ask people not to touch her, to leave her alone. Now, after the experience with these rotters, local hunters have taken it upon themselves to shoot strangers on sight. That's bad, of course. But I say, let them shoot. It turns out the local hunters knew about her existence long before I came along. Only they never told anyone. And they never encroached upon her territory themselves. The locals talked with her only when she came out to them. I started having pangs of conscience for having told about her without hiding the location, especially in the first edition of the book, and for not changing the names of people I mentioned, or even the name of the ship.

Anastasia calmed my fears a little when she said:

"Never mind. After all, I was the one who wanted to reveal myself to everybody."

But I'm wiser now. I shouldn't have mentioned specific names. And in future I shall try to be more circumspect.

But still I want to emphasise: *please don't disturb her.* She herself will tell everything she feels is necessary to reveal. We must not do to her what we have already done to one Siberian family — the Lykovs, described by Vasily Peskov in his *Komsomolskaya Pravda* article "Dead-end in the taiga". As far as I know, the only member of this family remaining is Agafia, who is dying of cancer, left helpless, taken out the taiga.[6] A real tragedy, how things have turned out. The Lykov family lived in the taiga for many years, but died out after contact with our 'enlightened' civilisation. Which way of life, then, is the "real dead-end"?

---

[5] This actually ended up being described in Book 3, rather than Book 2.

[6] *Agafia Lykova* — For the story of the Lykovs, see footnote 3 in Chapter 2: "Encounter". Since this book was published, Agafia's health has improved and she has returned to her original home, where she was recently visited by the original *Komsomolskaya Pravda* correspondent, Vasily Peskov.

I can understand why so many people want to contact Anastasia. But it is impossible for her to meet and talk with everyone. And, after all, Anastasia does have a young child.

There is an 'Anastasia' club or community organisation operating in Gelendzhik, headed by Valentina Larionova,[7] an ethnographer of thirty years' experience. She has organised a group of local ethnographers, along with people from a variety of professions, who are sensitive to the spiritual legacy of their region and its ecological problems. This was one of the first clubs to be organised by readers of the *Anastasia* book.[8]

The members of the Gelendzhik club have made what is to my mind a remarkable discovery. On the basis of information provided by Anastasia, they have restored to Russia — and, quite possibly, to the world — the forgotten shrines of our ancestors, and are now receiving people wishing to visit them and conducting tours to the places mentioned by Anastasia.

About Gelendzhik, for example, Anastasia had this to say: "This city could have been richer than Jerusalem or Rome, but because of its rulers' neglect of its primal origins this city is dying."

I believe this and other cities and settlements will be restored not by 'the rulers of this world' but by the hearts of ordinary people aroused by Anastasia.

And there's more. Anastasia is now the subject of conversation among many healers, wizards and preachers. "We are like ants compared to her," said the chairman of the Healers' Foundation Vladimir Mironov.[9]

[7]*Valentina Terentevna Larionova* — an ethnographer (and at one time a member of the Gelendzhik city council) who not only has taken special interest in the dolmens since the first publication of this book in Russian, but is one of the many who can bear personal testimony to the healing value of Anastasia's advice as set forth herein. More will be said about Ms Larionova in Book 2.

[8]*Anastasia* clubs have spread to many towns and cities in Russia and abroad, and since then have grown into a powerful social movement.

[9]*Vladimir Andreevich Mironov* — see footnote 6 in Chapter 27: "Across the dark forces' window of time".

I have seen a video recording of a speech given in front of a large audience by the leader of a religious denomination, in which he referred to Anastasia as "the ideal of womanhood to which we should aspire". He added: "Her ability to draw inferences and conclusions and level of intellect far surpasses that of our population today." This video is now being copied and distributed.

Much the same type of reaction is coming from people with extraordinary abilities living in India.

Still another religious leader said that while Anastasia is currently studying our life, she has not yet managed, unfortunately, to meet up with a real man. Later I was told that there is one chap very much like Anastasia living in Australia, and that the two should meet.

I, of course, do not have any pretensions to being a "real man", far from it, even in my thinking. But perhaps it is still premature to think in terms of arranging a marriage? And it isn't right to idealise her to such an extent.

It is this idealisation of Anastasia that has prevented a timely recognition of what she has done. Just think calmly and rationally about what has happened. A child has been born. And I have held him in my arms, I have heard his little heart beating. There is a child. He is growing up. But he has no official birth certificate. He will grow up and want to go somewhere — maybe abroad, for instance — maybe he'll want to see the world. Who will issue him a passport to travel abroad? What country is he a citizen of? What shall we tell him then? "Oh well, you know, somehow we haven't thought about any documents for you. You just stay here in the taiga."

I checked with a legal firm on the question of a birth certificate. The lawyer said Anastasia would have had to give birth in a hospital — then, even if she didn't have a medical record, they could have at least issued her a memo regarding the birth, which she could have used to obtain a proper birth certificate.

"The other alternative," said the lawyer, "would be for her to abandon her child to an orphanage. They would issue him documents there. Orphanages can do that. And then have him adopted." But somehow this alternative was not at all appealing. And I doubt that Anastasia would ever agree. So what to do? When I talked with her about a birth certificate, she responded:

"Of course, it would be fine if he had one, just like everyone else. I suppose I let that slip by without really thinking about it. But do not be concerned, everything will still work out."

Note how she said: "I suppose I let that slip by without really thinking about it." I wonder how many other things she has let 'slip by' — things which could be taken care of at a future stage. That means we can't fully count on everything working out exactly the way she said. I think we need to examine it all very carefully and at some point make adjustments to adapt it to *our* reality.

On another point, I hear talk about what a poor entrepreneur I am — not being able to print enough copies to keep pace with the demand!

Indeed. I really can't at the moment. I have refused to sell exclusive rights to the book to any one publisher. I certainly don't want anyone to have exclusive control over the manuscript and put out whatever print-runs they fancy.

The publishers I talked with gave me this: "...The style needs to be edited and made more literary. In its present form it is only Anastasia's explanations and monologues that make the book worth anything at all."

My language is seen as "stilted". They suggest I think up a catchier title — something like "Dead-end in the taiga", "The healer-girl", or even "The girl from outer space". But I do not consider Anastasia to be from outer space, nor do I consider her to be at a dead-end in the taiga. She herself, after all, simply wants to be Man, a normal human being. Of course I can always exercise my author's privilege even in confrontation with publishing houses, but a lot of time would be wasted on that.

I have been using the proceeds of the initial print-run to pay for subsequent runs in the print-shop,[10] by-passing the publishing houses altogether. So things will even out in the long run. If someone is interested in assisting along this line to our mutual advantage, I'd be happy to listen, but without the condition of exclusive rights.

---

[10] A reference to Moscow Printshop Number Eleven (see the end of Chapter 27: "Across the dark forces' window of time").

I should also say a few words about a certain situation involving my relationship with my family. The Moscow group now looking after distribution of the book has received a number of letters and telephone calls about this. There have been complaints that calls and letters to my home address indicated in the book have not been met with any intelligible response.

I left Novosibirsk, as I mentioned, directly upon my return from the expedition. Subsequent events will be described in my next book.

Now I have learnt that my firm is falling apart. And there has been nobody there to reply to enquiries. I'll see to it and bring it back to life once I finish my writing. As for my wife, I have only spoken to her on the telephone. It was a deeply personal conversation. However, I beg my correspondents' forgiveness for not responding right off and for my delay in sending out copies of the books.

At present my daughter Polina is there. I have met with her. She will fix everything up, and in future there should be no repetition of the trouble. I have had long talks with my daughter and she understands everything. A little later I plan to get a mobile telephone and then I shall be able to chat more personally.

I shall definitely respond to all the letters coming in and maybe even publish some of them. They are worth publishing. There are letters about Russia, about love, about bright aspirations. They show the same energy Elena Ivanovna Roerich[11] talks about in her book *Living ethics*. Thank you for these letters. But one letter in particular, a letter from a thirteen-year-old girl from Kolomna[12] named Nastia[13] deserves to be answered right here and now, along with other girls who have written and will be writing. Here is her letter:

Dear Vladimir Megre,
My name is Nastia Shapkina, from the city of Kolomna. I am 13 years old, and I am in Grade 7 at school. I read your book "The Ringing Cedar:

[11]*Elena Ivanovna Roerich* — see footnote 18 in Chapter 1.

[12]*Kolomna* — a city 100 km south-east of Moscow, where the Moskva River flows into the Oka.

[13]*Nastia* — a diminutive form of the name *Anastasia* (a common girl's name in modern Russian).

Anastasia". I really, really liked it. Not just 'liked' — that's not the best word here (it sounds too dry) — after reading the book I got a warm and happy feeling in my heart. They told me a lot about it in hospital — I've got a serious illness, and I have to go to hospital every two months, and I really want to get well. And your book was like a ray of light amidst all this darkness and vulgarity. I really want to meet with you, and especially with Anastasia. Could you help me?

Right now you're probably thinking: "How brash and impolite she is!", but that's not true. You see, that's the way we all are — until we see with our own eyes, we don't believe anyone. I don't even know whether to believe or not (Mama doesn't believe, and no one around here believes), it is so fantastic. And yet, why not? — to be honest, I believed, I really did, but all my friends keep saying "Fairy tale, fairy tale!" I'm confused. Please help me. I think you are a very brave man. You have written the truth — maybe you haven't yet told the whole story, but you've told a good part of it, that's for certain.

What happened between you and Anastasia — the way you offended her, and then it turned out she wasn't to blame — all sorts of things — yet still, I think, you shouldn't offend a person that way, even if, let's say, she's abnormal or a fake (but that's strictly my personal opinion — you may not agree with it).

Vladimir (sorry, I don't know your patronymic[14]), did Anastasia have a child or not, and if she did, is it a boy or a girl, and what did your wife think of that?

And my last question: you wrote that Anastasia's grandfather and great-grandfather rubbed the piece of cedar with their fingers, but you never said that Anastasia did this too. Did she really not do it, or did you just happen to leave it out?

Please answer me (I know you get whole bagfuls of letters, but please, just a few lines).

Good-bye!!!

Anastasia

---

[14]*patronymic* — see footnote 9 in Chapter 1. A child writing to an adult would normally use the combination of first name *plus* patronymic in addressing the adult.

Dear Nastia,

You will most certainly be a healthy, spiritually strong and pretty girl. I shall ask Anastasia the next time I visit her to help you. Yes, Anastasia has a unique approach to healing. She looks upon illness as a conversation between God and Man. An illness can be a warning or a deliverance from something even more terrible, and she showed me examples of this — I'll be telling about them later in a new book. I shall try and persuade her. Though she's pretty stubborn about sticking to her views. She says it's only Man himself, through his spirit and conscious awareness, who can cure anything without negative side-effects, while outside interference is often harmful.

Nastia, judging by your reaction to the book, you seem to be already healthier spiritually than a lot of people, and that's the main thing. I'm beginning to realise that that's really the case. As far as whether people around you believe or don't believe in Anastasia's existence, I'll answer you by quoting what someone said at one of my get-togethers with readers. When that question was put to me for the umpteenth time, he got up and declared in a loud voice: "Look, people! You're holding in your hands an impulse of inspiration, a thought bursting forth, a call to action, an idea! It's right there in your hands. What more do you want? A sample of her blood, urine and feces for analysis? Is there no way you can do without that? After all, the greatest and most important proof is already sitting right there in your hands!"

You see, Nastia, I've come to the realisation that Anastasia is an uncomfortable concept for many, and they'd rather she didn't exist at all. After all, she's breaking down a whole lot of technocratic theories, conventions and priorities. Against the background of purity emanating from her we suddenly start to become aware of our own filth, and that's not always what we want. Especially when we like to think of ourselves as so good and smart and conscientious, no matter what we do.

Anastasia said: "I exist for those for whom I exist."[15]

I didn't think there was anything special hidden in this statement. Anyone who wants to believe can believe. If they don't want to believe, they don't have to. However, I was mistaken. Some people read and nothing happens with them. Others... They find a great feeling of love, kindness and

---

[15] *I exist for those for whom I exist* — see Chapter 26: "Dreams — creating the future" above.

inspiration welling up in their heart. And, like a shower of spring rain, the world feels this grand poetry of love, a poetry of the heart which is capable of perceiving the light, magnifying it and sharing it with others. These are the people who feel her and know that she does exist.

As for my wife, Nastia, she reacted the way most women probably would. We've only spoken on the telephone. But my daughter Polina is ready to help me. She understands everything, and brings me letters. She was the one who brought me yours.

You say it was wrong on my part to offend Anastasia that way. Of course it's wrong. I would never do anything like that again. The same people can be different at different times.

Our son was born. He's such a strong little lad. Smiles all the time. And Anastasia is happy and enjoying her life.

My best to you, and to your Mama.

I wish you joy and happiness in your life. You deserve it.

You're a strong girl. And you can make your friends happier too, more consciously aware of things.

A word about religious believers — their enquiries and questions.

I have spoken about Anastasia with members of the clergy from our Russian Orthodox Church, as well as with representatives of various denominations. Some of them are quite favourably disposed to her. Others say, with some apprehension, that she's most likely a heathen — she could break down people's faith in religious doctrine, or resurrect idolatry or something nobody knows about yet — and it's wrong for her not to be baptised.

Her attitude to religion will be discussed in greater detail in the second book, and it is really quite extraordinary. I'll just mention a few points here.

"You see," she told me, "it is a good thing that they are already talking about the soul, about the good, the light. Who is the most worthy? I am unable to say."

"But what about the sects?" I countered. "The sects that have been banned. Now everyone says that they took the wrong path. Their actions were wrong."

"Do you think so? Then think of this: a group of soldiers is out on patrol. One of them in the lead has broken off or gone to one side and gets blown up by a mine. Yes, you can say: 'He took the wrong path, his actions were wrong.' But you can also say that these same actions saved other people's lives."

"In any case, Anastasia, which religion do you think is closest to you, the one most comprehensible?"

"Vladimir, let us say you had never seen your parents or talked with them. You would probably be happy to hear anyone talk about them. Even if they each talked about them a little differently. Where the truth lies, you can judge for yourself after reflecting on everything inside you. After all, you are their offspring, you are your parents' child. As for me, though, I do not need any intermediaries."

Well, okay. That's enough about doubts. There are some rather pleasant phenomena that Anastasia has somehow managed to bring about in our reality.

I was especially sceptical that she would actually be able to infuse something into the text of the book. These are her own 'combinations'[16] and rhythms, as she said, coming from the depths of eternity. But after the first edition came out, in a run of only four thousand copies, something incredible happened. Many people were so moved by feelings and emotions that poetic verses began flooding in all by themselves. There are a whole lot of them now. These are just ordinary people, not professional poets, who have been writing.

[16]*'combinations'* — see Chapter 27: "Across the dark forces' window of time" above.

There are enough poems to date to put out a whole separate volume of them.[17]

In the Moscow group devoted to studying Anastasia phenomenon, they say that nowhere in the world, in the past or present, has there ever been a person or figure capable of provoking such a huge poetic outpouring in so short a time.

Another surprising thing is that while in the first book there is almost nothing said about *faith*, or *Russia*, the majority of the readers' poems speak directly about faith and Russia, and bright aspirations. And it seems to me they do this most inspiringly. And this had a calming effect on my thought about Anastasia's influence. After all, the Bible tells us how to distinguish the bad from the good, the false prophet from the bearer of truth — it says "By their fruits ye shall know them."[18]

And if Anastasia's aspirations and her combinations bring forth such radiant poetic feelings, those are undoubtedly good fruits.

And I even thought: If this goes on much longer she's going to turn half the population of Russia into poets, enamoured of their Motherland, the Earth, and all Nature around them.

I sorted the poems into several categories: anonymous poems, signed poems, poems by soldiers and poems by government officials. And do you know what this kind of sorting shows?

It shows that there is absolutely no point in dividing society up the way we sometimes do, and blaming our troubles on certain categories of people — like entrepreneurs, the military, government officials. Their hearts all beat in exactly the same way, and across all these categories there are people sincerely striving for the light, for the good.

As for our troubles... They're something we probably all produce by ourselves.

In this edition of the book I have decided to publish one poem from each category.

---

[17]In the meantime, a 544-page volume of readers' poetry, art and letters has been published in Russian, under the title: *V luche Anastasii zvuchit dusha Rossii. Narodnaya kniga* (The soul of Russia sings in Anastasia's ray. A people's book).

[18]Matth. 7: 20 (*Authorised King James Version*).

1. ANASTASIA'S RAY

Into our busy, bustling life
Of lonely souls in crowds immersed,
From the vast Universe of Space
A Ray broke through to the Earth.

It glistened brighter than the light
Of the Sun or of gold of purest hue:
"My people! Greetings! Here I am
As your brother, speaking to you.

"I have been sent to you by love!
Sent to you by the ages' call.
Come to me and take of mine —
I give myself to all.

"Wait, there, my friend, where are you going?
Why is there sadness on your face?
You've been forsaken... Yes, I know...
I know all time and space.

"Dear people! What are you thinking, people?
The world is beautiful, no end.
I can do everything, dear people,
Because I am your friend!"

But the crowd only surged against the Ray,
Rushing along on their fashion-shod feet,
And kept on shoving it away
Into a puddle in the street.

The Ray dipped into the dirty slush...
It felt no offence, and shed no tear.
But all at once the slush burst forth
In a water-spring crystal-clear.

And then a little boy came running —
And fearing no punishment therefrom,
He leapt feet first into the puddle,
And drew on the Ray's sweet balm.

His Mama got angry with despair
And wildly waved her arms in dread,
But Pushkin's[19] statue on the square
Suddenly came to life and said:

"Now wait! You must not spank the boy!
He did not act just out of fun!
Pay heed to him — your hearts will be
Illumined by your son!

"Come near and feel his moistened hands,
Come close and touch your blessed son,
And you will find there in his palms
All that the poets have sung —

"All they've created through the ages —
Reflected there within the heart."
"Mama! Mainochka! My Mama!"
The little boy hugged his mum.

"Mama, can you hear the singing,
Hear the song of happy birds?
You know, dear Mama, yes, you know it.
I shall write you a verse.

"And now you will be happy, Mama.
For that is what I want for you.

[19]*Alexander Sergeevich Pushkin* (1799–1937) — Russia's best-loved poet, considered to be 'the father of Russian literature', to whom many a Russian poet since then acknowledges a debt of gratitude. His influence on the Russian literary language is comparable to Shakespeare's on English. He is immortalised in portraits and statues in hundreds of Russian towns and cities.

You see, I hear it, yes I hear it...
I think I can do it, too."

Into our busy, bustling life
Of lonely souls in crowds immersed,
From the vast Universe of Space
A Ray broke through to the Earth.

Author unknown

2. ANASTASIA (ANAS)

(on the image and heroine of V. Megre's book Anastasia*)*

In Russia Megre wrote this brand new idea
In book publications and newspaper lines,
The Ringing Cedar or *Ana-sta-si-ya,*[20]
Which drew attention to himself at the same time.

It's not the first time that this name I've heard spoken,
And yet it is still not that common a name:
Yes, *Ana-sta-si-ya* — so music-evoking,
Or *Stas-ya,* or *Stacie* — they all mean the same.
The Stacies I know live in cities of shadows,
Their character simple, of good honest worth
But here in the taiga, in a cedar-ringed meadow,
I glimpse a fair Goddess — the fairest on Earth.

---

[20] *Ana-sta-SI-ya* — see footnote 1 in Chapter 9: "Who lights a new star?". A diminutive form would be *STAS-ya* (*Stacie* in English). In this poem she is also called *Anas* (stress on second syllable).

Anas — a Siberian of Nature's creation —
In harmony with her environment lives.
Her conscious awareness, her love, inspiration,
To animals, plants, all around her she gives.

Her feelings and thoughts are in tune with the living,
The mind of the Cosmos is simple and clear.
In all of our wide world, believe me, there's nothing
Escaping her knowledge of stars or light-years.

Clairvoyant, Anas cures disease at all stages,
The great ringing cedar enhances her reach.
She draws upon cultures of all lands and ages
For logic and meaning and richness of speech.

An analyst practising Nature's ecology,
Her meaning of life is in tune with the world.
Intuitive grasper of highest astrology,
There's nothing impossible for this precious girl.

N. Mikhailov, Moscow

3. THE KIND WIZARD-GIRL

Gelendzhik's
Dolmens.
The years... wind back...
Time has opened a window, just a crack,
For the stretches of infinity
To be understood, evaluated,
Felt through and through, recognised as fact.
Stepping over my threshold-limit

Through the light of good in the blue expanses way up high,
I come to you, Anastasia,
Born again
In the twinkling of an eye!
You are a flower of Consciousness and Will,
Your might from cedar-trees and forest leaves,
And from such charming, mystical, magical thoughts
That I'm ready to be one who simply believes.
Every beast and insect, raven and jay,
Every serpent, blade of grass and hay,
You wizard-girl, kind maven of the way...
So many aroused by what you have to say...
Your thoughts, ideas, even stronger now today,
Shed light on all the Earth with their bright Ray!

O.T. Vialshina, Gelendzhik

4. ANASTASIA'S LOVE

To the woman of my beloved

I shall pray for you, for you are loved,
The woman of my own beloved,
As his heart's desire, you will be blest,
You will be blest, as I wished for you the best.

Keep him safe when he is strong, or weak, or brave,
Keep him safe when he may irrationally behave,
Keep him, keep my beloved safe and sweet,
My days, it seems, have flashed by in a beat,
Their crazy dance has burnt me with its heat,

My years have started passing all too fleet,
My son has started walking on his feet.

"Your Papa is the very best, my son,
The very best!
It is I who did not manage to open up to *him,*
In life, my son, that can happen on a whim,
Another woman takes his fancy and steps in."

You are both caressed by the gentle breeze of spring
Which tells me in the whisper of the leaves
How he feels the warmth,
How he feels the joy
Both from your hands
And from your lips.
I shall not dare distract him
From the warmth and tenderness of your eyes.

But should that not be enough,
I shall send you
A ray of sunlight
To relieve you of your grief.

The years will fly past
Just like a stormy night.
Life will seem to you like an empty room.
I, as a fading star, falling to Earth from above,
Shall chase from your soul the night-time gloom.
And I shall be able to pray, please do believe,
So that you, by the light-ray illumed,
Need feel no withering love,
I shall be able to pray, for you are loved,
The woman of my own beloved.

Author unknown

5. TO ANASTASIA

To a woman I dedicate this verse.
I write as an air force flyer.
A poet I could never be.
But my heart flared true.
My breast with fire did burst.
Anastasia!
Do not think me brash.
I can't stop loving you.
Your image, a touching pulse for good,
Pulsed louder than any engine ever could.
My engine failed... Visibility nil...
An explosion, in the twinkling of an eye...
But then your Ray of Light,
Your image, flashed and blessed,
On fragile wings it kept me in flight.
A single moment it took.
Only one. I wished — as I looked until
My landing gear touched safely down —
That I were a blade of grass upon the ground,
By your fingers tenderly caressed.

Author unknown

6. THE CEDAR FOREST RINGS AND CHIMES
To Vladimir Megre

Ah, the fragrance of Siberian cedars!
The smell of resin very strong
The taiga vast, almost half a globe sweeping,
Stretching to one grand endless song.

The cedars keep peace since times of old,
Maintaining the energy of the Earth.
To brighten the pulse-beat of the soul
They ring for all mankind these words:

"Here dwells among us Anastasia
In spiritual purity's forest art.
She watches over Mother Russia
Through people's holiness of heart.

"She sends out thoughts, and calls to action,
To the highway leading to heavenly light —
The essence of Veles, Krishna, Rama,
Shiva, Buddha, Allah, Christ.

"These holy thoughts, the Star-bright Logos —
Old Russian purity their theme —
Are flying like snowstorms, calling the ages
To penetrate to the heart of the dream.

"With me are forces of light, unchanging,
I exist for all who walk and plod.
I give to all a bright awakening
Who do not turn their back on God.

"Bow before Holy Russia's leading,
Bow to her Gods, our creators above —
In the never-ceasing ring of the cedars —
Which deify the light as love.

"So, Russians, turn! and with your soul
Pay heed to all that heaven gives:
On the rivers of Lena, Yana and Ob
God's Temple of all the Russias lives.

"Step out on the upward road to the light!
The Cosmic Self-Programming path discern!

We look to your goals, as you answer aright,
So Russia may to her Gods return.

"Preserver of the Cosmic energy of Nature,
The ringing cedar waits for the one
Who loves his Russia as God the Saviour,
Whose heart its course for others has run.

"Then live in peace and love for Nature,
Brook no dishonesty, live aright,
Draw wisdom's radiance from the people's favour,
And show to others the pathway to light!

"Such people are called by Anastasia
To accept my energy's gentle load,
So that the bright forces' attentive idea
May help those climbing up the road."

The cedars call everyone to hope for the prize
On the path to divinity, to beauty's gleam:
"Awaken, my people! Open your eyes!
Reach out to others, to the heart of the dream!"

The cosmic expanse opens wide its doors
To awakened pilgrims on their climb.
To those united on their upward course
The whole cedar forest rings and chimes.

Ya. N. Koltunov
President of the Cosmos Society
of the Russian Space Exploration Committee, Moscow

7. TWO GODDESSES

Do not come here to see my shame
Or think with mute reproach to bless:
Nor hand nor secret stare can claim
To lift the cross from my poor chest.

No earth-bound cry will scare away
The soul of heavenly confusion.
It will not blight the holy ray
Of mind and feeling's interfusion.
The world is full of sun and storm,
Of finger-snaps and love's fire too,
Here ashes, flame, blood, tears are born
Where mind is false, but feelings true!

Wild honey becomes bitter, surely —
No sweetness from the wormwood's bloom
Pretenders will not grasp the worldly,
The afterlife the wise will doom.

All stories, letters, poems, flowers,
Will waken to the heavenly blue!
I see two Goddesses, two powers:
These are my Poetry and You!

Verse should not be debased as phantom,
It will not see a final breath!
You are immortal, we are random
In poems, just like birth and death.

G. Pautov, physicist
Krasnodar

31

Author's message to entrepreneurs

The author's attempt to organise a fellowship of Russian entrepreneurs in accord with certain spiritual principles has revealed an evident desire for such a coming together on the part of many entrepreneurs. Notices were sent out all over Moscow. (A wider distribution throughout Russia would have entailed a substantial expenditure.) The lack of funding and, consequently, the ultimate failure of the project, led to nowhere. Anastasia's plans began to seem unrealisable.

During my second visit with her, however, she told me there were no dead-end situations, only that I should not have altered the sequence she had prescribed. The book should have come first, which would have spread the right information and prevented the organisational principles from being tied to monetary concerns.

This second visit also settled one other question. An organisational task force had been set up in Moscow to spearhead the formation of the fellowship, but we could not come to a decision on either the selection criteria for new members or how the selection committee should be constituted.

Anastasia stated the following:

"One's heartfelt impulse and one's aspiration to strive for such a fellowship are the principal criteria for eligibility. Nobody has the right to refuse access to anyone manifesting such qualities. One's past record is irrelevant. For the one who was most worthy yesterday may well turn out to be the least worthy today, and vice-versa. Subsequently, when you get together to determine the eligibility criteria according to the impulses of your hearts, you will also be able to work out the specific terms on which applicants are accepted into the fellowship."

The blame for altering the sequence prescribed by Anastasia falls, of course, on me. To all those Moscow entrepreneurs who wanted to join the fellowship I hereby offer my sincere apologies — first, for postponing the initial conference to a later date and, secondly, for the consequent drain on your time and finances.

The task force was indeed made up of dedicated entrepreneurs. Many of you had limited time to devote to the project. But you found the time, or stole it from something else, you worked on drafting documents and the principles for the future society. The secretariat too, similarly made up of Muscovites, was fuelled by enthusiasm. In addition, Moscow students put together a magnificent computer version of the future society's catalogue. It made it all the more painful for me to look back, once I realised my mistake, and see the hopelessness of the situation. The only way out was to muster the strength needed to correct the mistake and write the book. Without a word of explanation to anyone (explanations seemed impossible at that point!) I went off by myself and began to write.

It is only now that the book exists and is spreading more and more right across Russia and starting to fulfil the function specified for it by Anastasia that I can talk about the future. I am more confident now about the possibility of seeing such a society actually come into being.

The reaction to the book indicates that it will attract a sufficient number of entrepreneurs from the various regions of the country. The conference will take place. There will be a fellowship!

In acting on my own, I may well have offended some of those who worked alongside me in Moscow.

I should particularly like to single out three Moscow students[1] who gave their all to assisting and participating in the secretariat of the future society. They were the ones who keyboarded the text of the first book on their computers, and kept on keyboarding even after their exam session started. I wasn't in a position to compensate them for their work. They knew this, understood the situation, but still went on keyboarding. Others too would have probably reacted

---

[1] *three Moscow students* — see footnote 7 in Chapter 27: "Across the dark forces' window of time".

with understanding, had they known the whole picture. If that applies to any of you, I apologise for my lack of trust in you and for my temporary disappearance.

Of course there is a great deal more I need to learn and understand, including the degree to which Anastasia herself has been involved in all this. I'd like to know just how this reclusive young woman from the Siberian taiga managed not only to draw up plans like these but also to have them implemented in real life. It's not that she is predicting the future. She is literally creating the future, she struggles to bring it about and feels the struggle in her heart. In fact, it is something on the order of a master business plan which she has formulated in her head, keeping track of all its details down to the nuances of psychological probabilities. She is working her hardest to make it come about, and calling on us to participate in its realisation.

But we are not simply 'blind mice', but normal, professionally experienced adults, and we must understand that a single individual, especially one still relatively new to entrepreneurial practice, cannot foresee everything ahead of time.

Anastasia affirms:

"Just the organisation alone, the spiritual — yes, *spiritual* — contact among such people as entrepreneurs, is a salutary reaction of cosmic proportions. There is no need to dictate what will happen next. What will happen next will point out its own path and set its priorities in the occurrences of daily life."

What kind of reaction is this? What path is she alluding to?

Even though her aspiration to the light can be felt intuitively, nevertheless, we must make sense of everything ourselves and work out the details.

I wish you all happiness and success!

Dreams coming true
Editor's Afterword

In the summer of 1996 a tired-looking man was standing on a street corner in downtown Moscow, with a self-published 96-page volume in his hands, trying to sell it to passers-by. The book's title was *The Ringing Cedar. Anastasia*, and the man called himself Vladimir Megre.

A woman stopped by, looked at the inconspicuous cover, talked to the author and bought a copy. Next day she was back — smiling, her eyes shining — to pick up an entire pack, to give to everybody she knew.

As it was, the first print-run of 2,000 copies of *Anastasia* sold out in a matter of weeks. What happened next was as miraculous as the story Vladimir Megre had written down: new print-runs first of 2,000, then of 10,000, sold out within weeks. Not long afterward, *millions* more were printed and sold. By 1999 Vladimir Megre was one of Russia's most popular authors, and the seven books published to date have sold over 10 million copies in their original Russian alone, not counting their translated editions in more than a dozen languages.

The books in the *Ringing Cedars Series* started producing incredible changes in people's hearts and minds, the effect of which is now being felt throughout Russia and beyond. What happened here? How can it be that, with no advertisement other than word-of-mouth, this book by an unknown author became a national, then an international best seller, distributed initially by readers alone before it was accepted by even a single bookstore? How can it be that one copy from this first 2,000-copy print-run actually found its way to the stacks of the U.S. Library of Congress?[1]

---

[1]*Zveniashchii kedr: Anastasiia*, printed by Moscow Printshop Number Eleven in 1996, bears the Library of Congress Control Number 98171763. A copy from the first 1997 printing of Book 2, *Zveniashchie kedry Rossii* (The Ringing Cedars of Russia), has also been included in the Library of Congress collection (LCCN 98216313).

Why have people of all ages — from schoolchildren to pensioners — and in all walks of life — from teachers to public officials and from scientists to clergymen — felt such inspiration from the book to the point of writing poetry and creating works of art?

Why did a former member of the Russian parliament, an economist by the name of Dr Viktor Medikov, write an entire book, *Putin, Megre and Russia's future,*[2] stating that the Ringing Cedars was becoming Russia's new national idea?

Why did the Supreme Mufti[3] of Russia, Talgat Tajuddin, publicly declare in a televised interview: "I *love* these books. I read them and get a lot out of them for myself"? Why have leaders of other confessions made equally laudatory remarks?

Why did my mother once bring home a copy of *Anastasia* from her yoga class on the recommendation of her instructor, and gingerly request that I read it?

Why, when, applying to enter the doctoral programme in Forestry at six top-rated American universities, I submitted a research proposal based on the ideas set forth by Anastasia, I was accepted by all of them? Four of the schools, in fact, offered me full financial support with a scholarship. And here I am now at the University of Missouri at Columbia, writing my Ph.D. dissertation on the significance of ideas from the Ringing Cedars for the future of forestry and agriculture in Russia and the world as a whole.

But here comes the most striking part: how can it be that all these developments — from the wild popularity of the Ringing Cedars Series to the outpouring of reader's poetry and art — had been described in the very first book *before* coming to pass?

As it is, true to what Anastasia said in the very first volume, millions of people have been moved by her words, many thousands have planted trees, written poetry and songs, or created works of art — all inspired by the book. Readers' clubs have proliferated throughout Russia and abroad. Numerous readers' conferences throughout

---

[2] *Putin, Megre i budushchaia Rossiia*, published in 2003, is also found at the Library of Congress, with Control Number 2003710013.

[3] *Mufti* — a Muslim scholar who interprets *Shari'a* law.

Russia and Europe have brought together thousands of people, asking questions they had never even thought of before. In just the scant few years since the book's initial publication, Russia has witnessed the birth of a powerful eco-village movement, inspiring thousands of people to leave their jobs in large cities and, despite formidable obstacles, move to one of the many eco-settlements now sprouting all over the country. Russian emigrants to Germany, America and Canada have been flocking back to their homeland to establish new self-sufficient homesteads on their ancestors' lands. In the eco-village where my family now owns a plot of land, our neighbours include economists, singers, entrepreneurs, engineers, writers, mechanics, managers and executives, artists, peasants; young families, single mothers, pensioners and even schoolchildren — coming from all over Russia and other countries once part of the Soviet Union: from Moscow to Irkutsk and from Ivanovo to Kazakhstan and Tajikistan.

Whence comes all this inspiration?

The answer is simple: *Anastasia* resonates so strongly in tune with people's hearts that one cannot fail to inwardly recognise the truth emanating from it. How many times have I heard personal examples of this instant recognition: people who have been searching for years or decades for meaningful answers to questions on the purpose of life, on Man's place in Nature, have finally found them in this book!

But should it be surprising that the image of a way of life founded on the ideals of love, beauty and non-violence, as presented by Anastasia, would resonate so strongly with our inner self? After all, does not every one of us want to live in a free society of kind and happy people, in a world without wars, crime or oppression? In a world where not a single tear need run down a child's cheek, and where families live in love and prosperity? Do we not want to live without monstrous industries destroying and polluting both Nature and Man? Do we not want to enjoy creative labour for the benefit of both our families and our communities, instead of suffering through boring jobs merely to enrich faceless corporations? Do we not want a society based on mutual help and co-operation, rather than competition?

But, you may say, this was just Anastasia's *dream*. Or just Vladimir Megre's dream. And "a dream is simply a dream".[4] But cannot each of us dream of a desirable future and then act to bring this future about? Is it not what John Lennon was singing about in his *Imagine*:

You may say I'm a dreamer,
But I'm not the only one.
I hope someday you'll join us
And the world will live as one.

Is it not what one of the greatest economists of the twentieth century, E.F. Schumacher, was referring to in his seminal work *Small is beautiful?*[5]

Now, it might be said that this is a romantic, a utopian, vision. True enough. What we have today, in modern industrial society, is not romantic and certainly not utopian, as we have it right here. But it is in very deep trouble and holds no promise of survival. We jolly well have to have the courage to *dream* if we want to survive and give our children a chance of survival... [The crises of the industrial society] will become worse and end in disaster, until or unless we develop a new life-style which is compatible with the real needs of human nature, with the health of living nature around us, and with the resource endowment of the world.

Fortunately, the disaster may still be averted, as more and more people in Russia and throughout the world, drawing their inspiration from the Ringing Cedars, acquire "the courage to dream" and create an image of radiant reality for themselves and their children, and then get down to work in this direction.

The spiritual and practical revelations presented in this book are unparalleled in so many areas that their discussion could fill entire

[4]See Chapter 7: "Anastasia's ray".

[5]E.F. Schumacher, *Small is beautiful: Economics as if people mattered* (New York, Harper & Row, 1973), p. 162 (in the 1989 edition).

volumes. Let me but mention Anastasia's "beloved dachniks" — a discovery of exceptional significance.

As it happens, the most obvious and significant things often go the most easily unnoticed. This is particularly true about Russia's *dacha* movement. Judge for yourself — Anastasia and Vladimir Megre were the first to speak about the importance of *dachniks*. Now it turns out that according to widely available official statistics, published every year in Russia's primary statistical source *Rossiya v tsifrakh*, over 35 million families — and this amounts to 70% of the country's population — grow their own food on their plots and collectively provide far more vegetables, fruit, and even meat and milk than the whole country's commercial agriculture taken together.[6] Why had nobody paid attention to these numbers earlier? Why didn't they ever surface in the discussion on the present and future of Russian — and, indeed, the world's — agriculture? Why did nobody take seriously President Boris Yeltsin's confession that he was spending his weekends tending a vegetable garden, growing potatoes and radishes?

Should you choose to research for yourself the questions discussed by Anastasia, you will soon discover the truth of her assertion that *her* knowledge is already shared — at least partially — by a number of people in our world, and that "collectively they know practically everything, only they do not fully understand how it works".[7]

Take communication with plants, for example. It sounds incredible at first, but it only requires a reading of Peter Tompkins and Christopher Bird's well-researched *The secret life of plants*[8] to gain an entirely new perspective and conclude: She must be right!

But could it be possible that all diseases are curable through such interaction with plants, as Anastasia argues? It would take a complex and lengthy scientific study to test this hypothesis. Fortunately, this is not necessary, as — in addition to a growing number of personal testimonials from thousands of people — there is factual evidence

[6]The spiritual, social and economic significance of dacha movement is discussed in great detail in Book 5 of the series, *Who are we?* Dr Medikov referred to this book as "expressing Russia's new national idea".

[7]See Chapter 26: "Dreams — creating the future".

[8]New York: Harper & Row, 1973.

at hand that can dispel any doubts. Over centuries and millennia the Hunzakut, a people living in a valley in northern Pakistan, have been practising an agriculture very similar to the one described by Anastasia. Eating food *exclusively* from their family garden plots and thus establishing a closed loop of matter- and information-exchange between people and their plants, they are recognised as the most healthy and long-living people on Earth. The Hunzakut commonly live to more than 100 years, and men becoming fathers at age 90 is not a rarity.[9] Can it be that this information exchange between an individual person and a plant Anastasia talks about is the missing link to understanding human nutrition? Even in the absence of scientific studies, why not try it? The science will catch up.

Furthermore, why should we be sceptical about Anastasia's ability to live without concern for acquiring food or clothing — effortlessly relying on Nature for a complete life-support system? Is not the exact same ideal of life taught to humanity in the Bible: "He who watches the wind will not sow and he who looks at the clouds will not reap"[10] or "Take no thought for your life, what ye shall eat, or what ye shall drink".[11] Also, in our own not-so-distant past, Nobel Laureate Albert Schweitzer testified on the basis of his experiences in Africa: "In return for very little work nature supplies the native with nearly everything that he requires for his support".[12]

Looking around, should one doubt that truly happy children can *only* be raised in Nature? Jean Liedloff, who spent two and a half years in a society living in close relationship with Nature — and consequently knowing no such things as crying children, crime or depression — speaks about this in her book *The continuum concept*[13] with very much the same conclusions as Anastasia.

---

[9] See, for example, *Secrets of the soil* by Peter Tompkins and Christopher Bird (Yonkers, N.Y.: Rare Bird Press, 1998), or numerous other books written about the Hunzakut people.

[10] Ecclesiastes 11: 4 (*New American Standard Bible*).

[11] Matthew 6: 24 (*Authorised King James Version*).

[12] A. Schweitzer, *On the edge of the primeval forest: Experiences and observations of a doctor in Equatorial Africa* (London: A.C. Black, 1934), p. 112.

[13] London: Duckworth, 1975; rev. ed. 1977. From 1985 published by Addison-Wesley.

Again, this list could continue. In fact, researchers could — an
probably will — write volumes of commentary on almost every statement contained in *Anastasia*.

Yes, doubts naturally do creep in. It still sounds all too improbable to our traditional way of thinking. And even if the heart feels
a genuine light emanating from the book, the mind often refuses to
accept it as real. This is an all too familiar dilemma, fully experienced
even by Vladimir Megre himself. However, as the series progresses
and you come to embrace the ever more significant revelations set
forth in the subsequent volumes, and immerse yourself in their ever
more poetic language, the idea that it could all be "simply thought
up" should gradually melt away.

You hold in your hands a flower which will unfold its petals to reveal a most remarkable masterpiece, unique in all of Russia's literature and, possibly, the world's as well. Indeed, its significance goes far
beyond *literature*. This book possesses a tremendous, unprecedented
potential to change life on our whole planet for the better.

Do you know of any other book that in a matter of just a few years
has succeeded in not only stirring the hearts and minds of millions of
people, but also arousing these same people to extraordinary acts of
creation in their everyday lives, developing new modes of expression
in all the arts, taking or embracing non-violent initiatives to preserve
and enhance life on this planet as we know it? Every day more and
more people are joining in. Now that the Ringing Cedars is globally
available in English, the realisation of Anastasia's dream is certain to
take on planetary proportions. I have no doubt about it.

In the winter of 2003, at my office in downtown Moscow — just
one block away from the street corner outside the Taganskaya metro
station where Vladimir Megre had been selling the first copies of his
book only six years earlier[14] — Igor Vladimirov, head of the Anastasia
Readers' Club in St. Petersburg, mused one day, looking at the snow-
flakes dancing outside the window:

[14] At the time I was employed as Programme Manager at the Moscow headquarters
of WWF Russia — a branch of the World Wide Fund for Nature (also known in
America and Canada as the World Wildlife Fund) — just a five-minute walk from
the Taganskaya station. Megre's initial attempts to sell and promote his book are
painstakingly described in Book 2.

"Wouldn't it be wonderful to have *Anastasia* published in English?"

"It would," I agreed.

"You are a professional project manager, and you speak English fluently. Isn't that true?"

"Yes, more or less."

"Then *why are you sitting here?!*"

We laughed. A subsequent chain of circumstances and events led me to certain people — including Vladimir Megre himself — who became instrumental in carrying out the English translation project.

The story of the unusual co-incidences and struggles behind this edition could easily form the stuff of a suspense thriller (which I shall probably write one day). In the meantime I take comfort in the fact that you are now holding a masterfully translated volume in your hands. This alone is a good indication that dreams really do come true.

Columbia, Missouri, U.S.A.
January 2005   Leonid Sharashkin

Series at a glance

Anastasia, the first book of the Ringing Cedars Series, tells the story of entrepreneur Vladimir Megre's trade trip to the Siberian taiga in 1995, where he witnessed incredible spiritual phenomena connected with sacred 'ringing cedar' trees. He spent three days with a woman named Anastasia who shared with him her unique outlook on subjects as diverse as gardening, child-rearing, healing, Nature, sexuality, religion and more. This wilderness experience transformed Vladimir so deeply that he abandoned his commercial plans and, penniless, went to Moscow to fulfil Anastasia's request and write a book about the spiritual insights she so generously shared with him. True to her promise this life-changing book, once written, has become an international bestseller and has touched hearts of millions of people world-wide.

The Ringing Cedars of Russia, the second book of the Series, in addition to providing a fascinating behind-the-scenes look at the story of how *Anastasia* came to be published, offers a deeper exploration of the universal concepts so dramatically revealed in Book 1. It takes the reader on an adventure through the vast expanses of space, time and spirit — from the Paradise-like glade in the Siberian taiga to the rough urban depths of Russia's capital city, from the ancient mysteries of our forebears to a vision of humanity's radiant future.

The Space of Love, the third book of the Series, describes author's second visit to Anastasia. Rich with new revelations on natural child-rearing and alternative education, on the spiritual significance of breast-feeding and the meaning of ancient megaliths, it shows how each person's thoughts can influence the destiny of the entire Earth and describes practical ways of putting Anastasia's vision of happiness into practice. Megre shares his new outlook on education and children's real creative potential after a visit to a school where pupils build their own campus and cover the ten-year Russian school programme in just two years. Complete with an account of an armed intrusion into Anastasia's habitat, the book highlights the limitless power of Love and non-violence.

Co-creation, the fourth book and centrepiece of the Series, paints a dramatic living image of the creation of the Universe and humanity's place in this creation, making this primordial mystery relevant to our everyday living today. Deeply metaphysical yet at the same time down-to-Earth practical, this poetic heart-felt volume helps us uncover answers to the most significant questions about the essence and meaning of the Universe and the nature and purpose of our existence. It also shows how and why the knowledge of these answers, innate in every human being, has become obscured and forgotten, and points the way toward reclaiming this wisdom and — in partnership with Nature — manifesting the energy of Love through our lives.

Who are we? — Book Five of the Series — describes the author's search for real-life 'proofs' of Anastasia's vision presented in the previous volumes. Finding these proofs and taking stock of ongoing global environmental destruction, Vladimir Megre describes further practical steps for putting Anastasia's vision into practice. Full of beautiful realistic images of a new way of living in co-operation with the Earth and each other, this book also highlights the role of children in making us aware of the precariousness of the present situation and in leading the global transition toward a happy, violence-free society.

The book of kin, the sixth book of the Series, describes another visit by the author to Anastasia's glade in the Siberian taiga and his conversations with his growing son, which cause him to take a new look at education, science, history, family and Nature. Through parables and revelatory dialogues and stories Anastasia then leads Vladimir Megre and the reader on a shocking re-discovery of the pages of humanity's real history that have been distorted or kept secret for thousands of years. This knowledge sheds light on the causes of war, oppression and violence in the modern world and guides us in preserving the wisdom of our ancestors and passing it over to future generations.

The energy of life, Book Seven of the Series, re-asserts the power human thought and the influence of our thinking on our lives an the destiny of the entire planet and the Universe. Is also brings forth a practical understanding of ways to consciously control and build up the power of our creative thought. The book sheds still further light on the forgotten pages of humanity's history, on religion, on the roots of inter-racial and inter-religious conflict, on ideal nutrition, and shows how a new way of thinking and a lifestyle in true harmony with Nature can lead to happiness and solve the personal and societal problems of crime, corruption, misery, conflict, war and violence.

The new civilisation, the eighth book of the Series, is not yet complete. The first part of the book, already published as a separate volume, describes yet another visit by Vladimir Megre to Anastasia and their son, and offers new insights into practical co-operation with Nature, showing in ever greater detail how Anastasia's lifestyle applies to our lives. Describing how the visions presented in previous volumes have already taken beautiful form in real life and produced massive changes in Russia and beyond, the author discerns the birth of a new civilisation. The book also paints a vivid image of America's radiant future, in which the conflict between the powerful and the helpless, the rich and the poor, the city and the country, can be transcended and thereby lead to transformations in both the individual and society.

Rites of Love — Book 8, Part 2 (published as a separate volume) — contrasts today's mainstream attitudes to sex, family, childbirth and education with our forebears' lifestyle, which reflected their deep spiritual understanding of the significance of conception, pregnancy, home-birth and upbringing of the young in an atmosphere of love. In powerful poetic prose Megre describes their ancient way of life, grounded in love and non-violence, and shows the practicability of this same approach today. Through the life-story of one family, he portrays the radiant world of the ancient Russian Vedic civilisation, the drama of its destruction and its re-birth millennia later — in our present time.

To be continued...

Readers' reviews

Yes, at last, truth that has not been distorted by dogma or someone's ego! I might explode from emotion if I read any more! I had a hard time getting myself to just stand still. I was jumping all over my garden saying hello to all my trees. (I've always talked to trees but I didn't know they were listening!) I then ran off and bought loads of seeds and spent days putting whole packets of them in my mouth, only to get very sick indeed, for little did I know that seeds bought in a supermarket are covered in rat poison! Have we gone mad?

I've got this strange reputation of a person who lives in a pink world, a dreamer believing in an unrealistic utopia of happiness, a witch, a madwoman... Well thank you Anastasia, finally I can take my place as just a normal Man, a woman. I'm so excited, fancy me not knowing that there was a whole bunch of 'pink worlders', just around the corner!

Vladimir is a true hero. He went all the way to the bottom of despair and he used his suffering to change. Merit and achievement, success and glory belong to those who have managed to change the most in their lives.

— *Ana, Portugal*

In 1996 I spent a day in the Australian bush with an aboriginal woman. This was my first encounter of what I call a 'natural human'. Her connectedness with nature blew me away and I wanted that for myself and all mankind. Likewise, Anastasia is in total harmony with nature and gives practical steps to rekindle in us that which is our true essence. I cannot even begin to describe the depth of the effect Anastasia has had on me and I have only read Book 1. For the first time in my life I feel affirmed on a very deep level and feel free to be me. I am so excited to have discovered these books and am fully committed to doing what I can to help spread their message.

— *Mary Dwen, New Zealand*

I truly found lots of inspiration in the book. I have a lovely garden plot which I have worked for over 40 years in the suburban Denver area and while I have tried to work with Nature 'consciously' for probably twenty years, I feel I fall quite short of anything that resembles the connection that Anastasia has. I am determined this next spring to do it exactly as she recommends because I do feel that humanity's healing will only come about with a reconnection to Nature. I am hopeful of many people also wanting to read the messages of hope and re-discovering the potential that awaits Man as he reclaims his Divine Inheritance through Right Action and Right Use of Will, attuned to Spirit!
— *Aurelia, Colorado, USA*

Anastasia and subsequent volumes tell the story of a return of mankind to a state of grace through love, actualizing real love to everything around us and keeping our thoughts, hearts, minds in the place of love, touching with love the earth and celebrating the God's creation through loving it and caring for it. I think the most important lesson for us is to move back to the work of the Creator and away from ways which destroy it. That is what I take from the Series and find myself inspired to work harder and being joyous, thankful and loving.

In my own life, our family works toward goals that aren't measured in dollars, which is a much richer life than working for material wealth. We have a certified organic and wild crops farm, so I am very receptive to the medicines of the earth and see the importance of people interacting in a healing way with God's Creation — the earth. In a very humble way, our work with native plants on our farm could be seen as demonstration of a way people can take some of the Ringing Cedars ideas and put them to work.

I think if people find a larger purpose for their lives than collecting material goods, everyone will be happier rediscovering the scope of humanity's tools from the Creator. *Anastasia* helps with explaining ways to have a richer life, raise healthier children, filling one's heart rather than one's pockets. I do not agree with everything written, and many people will find ideas threatening. Yet if we don't discover new ways of being human beings and put them to work, if we don't have a spirit rich enough to live with love and respect for God's creations, we have no future.
— *Penny Frazier, Missouri, USA*

There has been a very significant change taking place within me since reading the Series. It has been a casting off of the selfish elements within me and walking into a vast chasm of blessings. What is possible I do not yet know, only that an awareness and a consciousness is possible in this life. My life is hopeful now.
— *Allan, Wisconsin, USA*

At work I walked by a book lying face down on a messy table and it called me. I picked up the book, flipped it over and the cover clicked. I sat down and started reading. That night I took the book home and over the next few days I found a piece of life, of the spiritual cosmos, which I knew had been missing.

In my disgust and shame at Vladimir Megre's reaction to Anastasia, I saw a reflection of my own attitudes towards concepts I was uncomfortable with. Although Anastasia herself is a little odd, I had no difficulty believing in her presence, her existence. After reading the book, I slept under the stars, near some current bushes, but some possums awoke me in the middle of the night. I then did some reiki and sent the energy to Anastasia, and felt myself floating in cedar branches, softly brushing me, with a bright yet soft ball of radiant light shining back upon me. In a tarot read I asked about Anastasia and drew the Guardian card.

Three years ago my family moved to the country, our own *dacha*. I now look forward to next spring and "coding" the seeds and creating a space of love for both my garden and my family.
— *Dietrich Jakobi, Missouri, USA*

Anastasia's messages throughout the Ringing Cedars Series have further illuminated the Divine work of birthing, caring for, and parenting children. I am a *doula*, a home-birth mama, a dancer-singer who has been inspired by Anastasia's reminder that we all are born to know and share our Light.

I feel like the book's messages have found a natural home in my being. Anastasia is a being who I know lives, and she desperately wants us to feel how ALIVE we are and how ALIVE the Earth is. We belong to the Earth, and we must find our happiness so that the Earth will feel her happiness as well.
— *Elise, Missouri, USA*

My acquaintance who paid a visit to the Altai several years ago, receiv
a few tiny scraps of cedarwood from a local woman. She told him
wear it on his body: he would need it, it would protect him. This sum
mer he did some major 'housecleaning', sorting things he didn't want
around anymore. He stumbled on a matchbox with these slivers of
cedarwood, and thought: ah! is this true or mere superstition, shall I
finally do away with them? The next day, by 'coincidence', his friend
offered him the *Anastasia* book as a present. He read, gasped and made
a pendant out of the pieces. A few weeks later he showed me the pendant and it was breathtaking! I really gasped for breath, even though
at that point he hadn't yet told me his story. My guess would be that he
received some shivers of a ringing cedar — it was so moving to see it...
Many more stirrings over here, really trust that this will be worldwide.
— *Dickie, Netherlands*

As a 75 year-old American who finished the third *Anastasia* book by
V. Megre, *The Space of Love*, I am in the process of digesting its substance.

The American must pick up and go to a place that Vladimir Megre
shows him. Megre shows him wonders. But those expecting wonders to be valid only if found on American soil will be taken aback to
learn they are in a land that rarely thinks of the *New World*.

Anastasia's Siberian taiga is a land that measures history in millennia instead of decades. There, Vladimir meets those who have a mystical affection for their country and culture. He finds values resting
on rock-solid Christian principles not bearing Christian labels. They
are values descending from ancient insights, approved by generations
faithful to the soil of their forbearers. Their love for *Mother Russia* is
a love not understood even by the most patriotic American.

Christians will recognize much from the *Old Testament* as well as from
the *New*, especially *Isaiah*, Chapter 11. This is not to say the *Anastasia*
Series promotes or detracts from that teaching. Instead, it parallels and
edifies. The Christian emerges with his faith firmer and a respect for
Megre's *Anastasia*... After three books, I am digesting, and there are moments when my credulity vanishes. Then, lines appear that can have been
written *only* to me. Then my unbelief is overturned. It is like the story of
Lazarus. I believe, but help my unbelief! Coincidences are endless.
— *Gallagher Rule, Ponca City, Oklahoma, USA*

...UT THE RINGING CEDARS SERIES

...1994 a Siberian elder told entrepreneur Vladimir Megre a fascinating ...ory about 'ringing cedars' — sacred trees which heal bodily diseases and ...levate the human spirit. The elder told him where such a cedar was growing in the Siberian backwoods. Intrigued, Vladimir Megre delved into literature on Siberian cedar trees and was one of the first Russian businessmen to re-discover the tremendous folk medicinal, nutritional and commercial value of virgin oil pressed from Siberian cedar nuts. However, knowledge of the traditional technique of pressing the oil had been lost.

Determined to re-discover the secret and launch a highly lucrative production of cedar nut oil, Vladimir Megre set out on an expedition to find the tree, but his encounter with the elder's granddaughter, named Anastasia, transformed him so deeply that he abandoned his commercial plans and, penniless, went to Moscow to fulfil his promise to Anastasia and write a book about the spiritual insights she so generously shared with him.

What happened next has thrilled and inspired millions. With no advertisement other than word of mouth, books of the RINGING CEDARS SERIES have sold over 10 million copies in Russia alone and have been translated into 20 languages, making Vladimir Megre one of Russia's most widely read authors. Inspired by the Ringing Cedars, thousands of people are now planting trees, changing their lifestyle and, in search for a mortgage-free existence and spiritual re-connection with the Earth, are relocating to new eco-villages which have sprouted all over Russia and beyond. Thousands of readers have felt a huge creative upsurge and started writing poetry and songs and doing paintings.

These mind-stirring books read like a fascinating novel, have the authenticity of a documentary account and present spiritual insights of incredible depth. As books that address issues in which all our way of living and thinking is involved, they cannot be confined to a single category. Spanning dozens of subjects from child-rearing to gardening, from adventure to the meaning of human life, from megalithic science to breast-feeding and from sexuality to religion, they reassert the limitless creative potential hidden in each of us and present an incredibly beautiful and equally practicable vision of humanity's spiritual connection to Nature that helps us understand ourselves and heal our Earth.

Vladimir Megre could not know that his 1994-95 trade trips would change his entire life and affect the whole of humanity. Anastasia's messages have spread like wildfire throughout Russia and beyond. News reporters are already writing about a "new dawn" unfolding and an "eco-village revolution" taking place, which may change the country's — and the whole world's — destiny. Read these books and witness the birth of a radiant vision that has changed our life and may change yours.

THE AUTHOR, Vladimir Megre, born in 1950, was a well-known entrepreneur from a Siberian city of Novosibirsk. In 1995 — after hearing a fascinating account about the power of 'ringing cedars' from a Siberian elder — he organised a trade expedition into the Siberian taiga to rediscover the lost technique of pressing virgin cedar nut oil containing high curative powers, as well as to find the ringing cedar tree. However, his encounter on this trip with a Siberian woman named Anastasia transformed him so deeply that he abandoned his business and went to Moscow to write a book about the spiritual insights she shared with him. Vladimir Megre now lives near the city of Vladimir, Russia, 240 km (150 miles) east of Moscow, devoting himself to writing. Following the runaway success of his Series, he has spoken at readers' conferences throughout Russia and Europe, as well as established the Anastasia Foundation, a non-profit organisation aimed at promoting the ideas contained in the books and providing support to Russia's nascent eco-village movement.

THE TRANSLATOR, John Woodsworth, originally from Vancouver (British Columbia), has forty years of experience in Russian-English translation, from classical poetry to modern short stories. For the past twenty-three years he has been associated with the University of Ottawa in Canada as a Russian-language teacher, translator and editor, most recently as a Research Associate and Administrative Assistant with the University's Slavic Research Group. A published Russian-language poet himself, he and his wife — poet and amateur artist Susan K. Woodsworth — are directors of the Sasquatch Literary Arts Performance Series in Ottawa. Now a Certified Russian-English Translator, John Woodsworth is in the process of translating the remaining volumes in Vladimir Megre's Ringing Cedars Series.

THE EDITOR, Leonid Sharashkin, is writing his doctoral dissertation on the spiritual, cultural and economic significance of the Russian *dacha* gardening movement, at the University of Missouri at Columbia. He also travels across America and internationally, speaking about The Ringing Cedars Series and its global impact. After receiving a Master's degree in Natural Resources Management from Indiana University at Bloomington, he worked for two years as Programme Manager at the World Wide Fund for Nature (WWF Russia) in Moscow, where he also served as editor of Russia's largest environmental magazine, *The Panda Times*. Together with his wife, Irina Sharashkina, he has translated into Russian *Small is beautiful* and *A guide for the perplexed* by E.F. Schumacher, *The secret life of plants* by Peter Tompkins and Christopher Bird, *The continuum concept* by Jean Liedloff and *Birth without violence* by Frederick Leboyer.

ORDERING INFORMATION

USA and Canada:
- *order on-line* — www.RingingCedars.com
- *order by phone / fax (toll-free)* — 1-888-DOLMENS (1-888-365-6367)
- *e-mail* — sales@RingingCedars.com

New York, USA:
- *order on-line* — www.RingingCedarsUSA.com
- *order by phone (toll-free)* — 1-877-540-6742
- *e-mail* — sales@RingingCedarsUSA.com

Australia:
- *order on-line* — www.RingingCedars.com.au
- *order by phone* — 0414-327-000
- *e-mail* — sales@RingingCedars.com.au

New Zealand:
- *order on-line* — www.RingingCedars.co.nz
- *order by phone* — 64-9232-9792
- *e-mail* — sales@RingingCedars.co.nz

United Kingdom:
- *order on-line* — www.RingingCedars.co.uk
- *e-mail* — sales@RingingCedars.co.uk

Washington, USA:
- **Lemuria**, 303 First Street South #2, Yelm, WA 98597
- *phone* — 360-458-2699
- *e-mail* — francesca@ywave.com

The English translation of the Ringing Cedars Series may be ordered directly from the publisher, **Ringing Cedars Press**

www.RingingCedars.com

with delivery world-wide, and from a growing number of distributors and bookstores in cities, regions and countries around the globe. Generous discounts are available on a purchase of multiple copies of the same title. To become a distributor or to order bulk quantities of the books, please e-mail

distrib@RingingCedars.com